"With each turn of the page, you realize with increasing urgency how necessary and important this book is. Applying a journalist's eye to the language of faith, Jonathan Merritt breathes new life into familiar words and phrases, expertly employing history, etymology, biblical studies, survey data, and personal narrative to show that how we "speak God" really matters. Smart, eclectic, and delightfully readable, *Learning to Speak God from Scratch* is packed with little gems of knowledge and insight that will get you thinking. It deserves a place of honor on the bookshelf of every writer, every pastor, and every person of faith who understands that, as Mark Twain put it, 'the difference between the almost-right word and the right word is . . . the difference between the lightning bug and the lightning.'"

—RACHEL HELD EVANS, *New York Times* best-selling author
of *Searching for Sunday* and *Inspired*

"Am I the only Christian who doesn't (want to) speak 'Christianese'? Tell me about your relationship with God, and I'm all ears. But preach to me about the 'secular world' or how when 'God closes a door, he opens a window,' and I'm looking for a window to jump out of. As a television personality, there is so much at stake when it comes to the language of faith, and the last thing I want to do is lose the understanding of my spiritual experiences because of a vocabulary that is not relatable. In *Learning to Speak God from Scratch,* Jonathan fills this awesome book with entertaining stories and clever tools for speaking God more freely. Aah . . . insert praise hands emoji."

—JEANNIE MAI, TV personality and cohost of the
The Real on Fox

FOREWORD BY SHAUNA NIEQUIST

LEARNING TO SPEAK GOD FROM SCRATCH

Why Sacred Words Are Vanishing—
and How We Can Revive Them

JONATHAN MERRITT

CONVERGENT
NEW YORK

Library of Congress Cataloging-in-Publication Data
Names: Merritt, Jonathan, author.
Title: Learning to speak God from scratch : why sacred words are vanishing—and how we can
    revive them / Jonathan Merritt.
Description: New York: Convergent, 2018. | Includes bibliographical references.
Identifiers: LCCN 2017054862 | ISBN 9781601429308 (pbk.) | ISBN 9781601429315
    (electronic)
Subjects: LCSH: Christianity—United States. | Christianity and culture—Religious aspects—
    Christianity. | Communication—Religious aspects—Christianity. | Language and
    languages—Religious aspects—Christianity. | Christianity—Terminology.
Classification: LCC BR517 .M474 2018 | DDC 261.0973—dc23
LC record available at https://lccn.loc.gov/2017054862

ISBN 978-1-60142-930-8
Ebook ISBN 978-1-60142-931-5

Printed in the United States of America

Book design by Karen Sherry
Cover design by Mark Ford

Interior infographs by Summer Verwers/Lemon Whistle Media. Copyright © Jonathan Merritt.

10 9 8 7 6 5 4 3 2 1

First Paperback Edition

Contents

Foreword by Shauna Niequist ix

0 Struck Mute in a Strange Land 1

──────────── THE LOST LANGUAGE OF FAITH ────────────

1 Sacred Words in Crisis 15
2 Why Speaking God Matters 33
3 Our Divine Linguaphile 43
4 The Possibility of Revival 51
5 How (Not) to Speak God 59
6 The Way Forward 72

──────────── FINDING OUR VOICES AGAIN ────────────

7 Yes 85
   Sacred Affirmations and Necessary Nos

8 Creed 92
   Heresy Hunters and Twitter Farewells

9 Prayer 100
   Folded Hands and Brain Scans

10 Pain 106
   Chronic Conditions and Other Metaphors

11 Disappointment 112
   Dopamine Roller Coasters and Palm Branches

12 Mystery 124
   Apologetics, Addictions, and Infinite Knowability

13 God 127
   Tattooed Jesus and a Full-Narrative Deity

14 Fall 133
Scientific Quandaries and the Beauty of You

15 Sin 136
Pocket Nails and a Mountain of Metaphors

16 Grace 143
Umbrellas and Unmerited Favor

17 Brokenness 147
Reparative Therapy and Our Aversion to
Responsibility

18 Blessed 152
Hollow Hashtags and Marble Toilets

19 Neighbor 156
Mister Rogers and the Global Refugee Crisis

20 Pride 164
The Self-Esteem Movement and Tiptoe Terms

21 Saint 168
Protestant Holes and Holy Fools

22 Confession 172
Internet Vulnerability and Grace the Doorman

23 Spirit 178
Mr. Ghost and the Pronoun Wars

24 Family 184
Our Changing Households from Munsters to Dunphys

25 Lost 192
Microaggressions and Our Common Condition

+ In the Beginning Was the Conversation 198

A How-To Guide for Seekers and Speakers 205

Recommended Reading for God-Speakers Everywhere . . . 208

Acknowledgments 211

Notes 213

Foreword

I began learning French when I was seven, and that sparked a love affair with linguistics that continues still. I'm fascinated by the way different cultures name and identify things. I love to learn new words. I am enchanted by foreign languages. And when I meet a person with an unusual name, to my family's eternal mortification, I always ask how it's spelled and where it came from, so that I can visualize it written and understand its etymology.

I cannot express to you how delighted I was when I learned the French phrase *l'esprit d'escalier,* which literally translated means "stairway wit," but represents thinking of the perfect retort only after you've left the room. Another favorite, the German word *kummerspeck,* refers to excess weight gained from emotional eating—literally, "grief bacon."

Most writers I know would call themselves "word people." I certainly am one. The letters, the sounds, the way words appear on a page—this is pure magic to me. I can write five bad pages and then one sentence that pleases me, and everything is redeemed.

But my love for language goes beyond my work. As a Christian, I'm fascinated by the words we use when we talk about faith. It seems to me there are several words we've overused, and in doing so stripped them of their meaning. Some give you away as a southerner or a Calvinist or a King James Bible reader. Others signal a Pentecostal bent or years spent in Catholic school. And many have become dog whistles: words that most people hear innocuously, which Christians hear in an entirely different way. There is a troubling amount of jargon—words that we *kind-of-sort-of* understand but are mushy, imprecise, careless.

This is both fascinating and tricky. How do we sift through all the denominational and historical and regional inspeak to communicate meaningfully about something as both universal and deeply personal as God? How do we restore some important words back to their richest and most precise meanings, so that we can elevate our language about God? How do we widen some words that have been narrowed, and how do we redefine some that have been mangled far beyond a simple tweak?

This is what my friend Jonathan has done with elegance and intelligence. I'm so thankful for his love of language and for the precision and depth with which he has approached this topic. For every lover of words, for every Christian who has lamented the deterioration of the language of faith, for every devout individual who has struggled to be understood by someone from another tradition, for every one of us who is desperate to communicate beyond a field of faith words that are cliché-ridden and vague, this book is good news.

Words shape and precede action, and words act as the building blocks of communication. Here is another way to say it: words are the starting point both for who we become and how we connect. What could be more important?

Every "word person" loves the creation account in Genesis where God *speaks* things into being. This makes sense to us—we know it to be true, on the page and in life. Words are much more than vocabulary, and the way we use language has implications far beyond grammar. Our language is connected to our living in a thousand ways.

So *Learning to Speak God from Scratch* will not just challenge you to speak more intentionally but also to live more fully. This book will help you speak God anew as well as empower you to embody those words.

Better yet, in an increasingly disconnected and contentious age, this book will restore hope for the possibility of shared language, and with it, shared understanding. A revived vocabulary of faith represents to me a beautiful and important thing: a renewed ability to connect with our neighbors and friends about religious identity and practice, a meaningful bridge building.

I encourage you to read this book with pen and notebook in hand, writing yourself a new vocabulary of devotion. When you turn the final page, I hope you gather together with people you love to begin a new conversation about God, fresh with meaningful and weighty words. And I hope that across these pages, Jonathan becomes a friend to you the way he has been to me—someone who keeps calling us back, both to deeper language and to a deeper faith.

—Shauna Niequist
New York Times best-selling author of *Present over Perfect*

Many adults hunger for meaning and goodness, but lack a spiritual vocabulary to think things through.

David Brooks

A lot of the words we need the most have been watered down by overuse and cliché in politics and culture, and this includes words that are very meaningful for many Christians: *love, peace, faith,* and *justice,* to name a few. I don't think we can expect these words to necessarily convey what we mean when we say them, and so we must surround them with an ecosystem of vocabulary—and both words and practices—to carry the richness of our meanings when the words themselves need reviving.

Krista Tippett

Struck Mute in a Strange Land

A life coach once told me that adults searching for meaning should pursue their childhood dreams. Which seems reasonable enough if you fantasized as a kid about becoming a tax attorney or insurance adjuster. The principle doesn't work as well for people like me, who dreamed about becoming a cowboy.

My mother reminisces about the way I played pretend in the living room, wearing nothing except pajama bottoms, a mini Stetson hat, and black boots with silver spurs. I'd force my cowboy boots onto the wrong feet, which made the whole scenario a little more precious and a lot more absurd. On more than one occasion, I sauntered around the house, knock-kneed, waving a plastic six-shooter and asking where I could find a good watering hole.

"When I grow up," I told my mother, "I'm movin' to El Paso."

I had never been to El Paso. Heck, I'd never even seen pictures. In my version of El Paso, the townsfolk rode horses and never left home without pistols strapped to their hips. Only one lawman lived there, and he could usually be found outside the jailhouse smoking a hand-rolled cigarette. I assumed most residents wrangled cattle during the day, lay under a blanket of stars at night, and after a hard week's work, gathered at the saloon for a frothy mug of sarsaparilla and a hand of Texas Hold 'Em.

When I was old enough to move to the city of my choosing, however, El Paso didn't even make the Top 10. My cowboy dream had long faded.

When I decided at the age of thirty-one to join the 8.5 million city slickers who call New York City home, I wondered if that wrangler spirit had led me there.

You won't find horses in the Big Apple unless they're dragging carriages around Central Park. The only cows we have are served medium rare and will cost you a second mortgage. The city's strict gun laws mean you're unlikely to see a pistol unless it's resting in a police officer's holster, and the closest thing you'll find to a tumbleweed is a windswept potato chip bag.

And yet, New York City has a certain frontier-like quality. Countless people arrive each year—in moving vans, like modern covered wagons—with hopes of forging a new life, conquering the iron wilderness, and if they're lucky, maybe even striking gold. The scent of opportunity is everywhere—I've caught whiffs on street corners and nearly choked on it on Wall Street.

America's biggest metropolis is diverse enough that citizens can curate their own version. The New York of the Upper East Side is not at all like the New York of Astoria, Queens. So different are the two neighborhoods that it's almost laughable for them to claim the same city of residence.

I settled into the Brooklyn neighborhood of Williamsburg, which is less like *Seinfeld* and more like *Blue Bloods*. The buildings are smattered with graffiti and bursting with third-wave coffee shops. Hipsters and Latinos mingle with a remnant population of Hasidic Jews who have decided to stay put even as the neighborhood gentrifies. (I spy more menorahs during Hanukkah than twinkling trees at Christmas.)

On the waterfront, Brooklyn residents lounge with loved ones on benches beside the East River and watch the summer sun sink into the skyline. The final rays of dusk wash Manhattan's skyscrapers with sheets of light on clear nights. During the autumn months, McCarren Park fills with guitarists and flag football teams and a weekend farmers' market where you can purchase apple cider and tupelo honey and rhubarb jelly.

Living here is just as lovely as it sounds.

The delights of New York did not blindside me, of course. But I never anticipated, upon arriving, that I'd run into a crippling language barrier. Sure, I could order a late-night kabob from a halal street cart or relay an address to a taxicab driver. I spoke English as well as I always had.

My problem was that I could no longer "speak God."

Prior to moving to New York, I resided in a suburban neighborhood in the heart of the Bible Belt. Almost all my friends were Christian, and most of us attended the same type of church. I worked as a minister to a congregation outside of Atlanta, and before that, I was a full-time seminary student. The community in which I was immersed was so thoroughly Christian, I sometimes forgot that other people practiced different religions or none at all.

In this world, there was a kind of cultural Christian lingo that most speak and almost everyone else understands. If someone sneezed, a stranger might say, "God bless you." The sneezer would not stop to think, *What do you mean by "God"? Or by "bless"?* If someone mentioned that he had been "saved," "born again," or "attended a Bible-believing church," no follow-up question was needed. On meeting a new acquaintance, southerners will usually ask *where* they attend church rather than *if.*

I used religious language with ease in the South, rarely pausing to think about the meaning of my words. I grew up surrounded by these syllables of faith, used daily in my home and community. But I was not in Georgia anymore. I penned columns about the intersection of "faith and culture" from my southern Christian enclave, but as it turns out, pontificating about a post-Christian society is far easier than living in one.

In New York, religious fluency is not assumed. The majority of residents don't attend church on any given Sunday, and only about 3 percent of the population is evangelical Protestant like I was raised.[1] I soon discovered people who had never heard the sacred words I'd long taken for granted—and others who used them with wildly different meanings.

I realized this linguistic chasm en route to visit a church in Manhattan on my first Sunday in New York. Waiting on a subway platform, a woman standing next to me asked where I was headed. I explained that I was going to a "worship service." She asked for clarification, having never heard that phrase. I clarified that I was new to the city and was going to visit a church. She perked up and said she practiced the Baha'i faith. She held up her crystal amulet necklace and explained that it protected her from evil spirits. If I was spiritually curious, the woman said, she'd read my chakra and access the invisible energy fields around my body.

As we talked about our respective religious practices, it became clear that neither of us understood what the other was saying. I glanced down the dark tunnel in hopes of spotting a train, but rescue wasn't in sight.

She peppered me with questions about God and the Bible and the afterlife. I fumbled for answers, but what came out didn't make much sense. When I used terms I considered common—"grace" or "gospel" or "salvation"—my conversation partner stopped me midthought to ask for a definition, please. I sputtered, stammered, and stuttered, trying to rephrase those words in ordinary vernacular, but I couldn't seem to articulate their meanings. It was like trying to define the word *color* or *the*. Though I had used the terms often, I'd never stopped to consider their meanings.

The train finally slid into the station. I thanked the woman for conversing, though I felt anything but grateful, and bolted down the platform to find a separate train car.

Not all New Yorkers are like this woman, I came to realize. Others presented a different set of obstacles. Many are familiar with sacred terms but have experienced them as a source of pain or judgment or coercion. In such cases, I often felt embarrassed to speak the vocabulary of faith.

When a new friend in my co-working space asked me whether I was like the hypocritical Christians he saw on television shamelessly stumping for politicians, I was drenched in shame. But I could understand his contempt.

Terms like *sin* and *hell* have become so negative they lodge in our throats. Others, like *belief* and *salvation* have been uttered so often we don't know what they mean anymore.

The way certain groups of people use sacred words gives the rest of us the holy heebie-jeebies.[2] Holy phrases become tools of manipulation in the hands of angry religious leaders. They are fashioned into clubs by combative evangelists. And when shouted from the mouth of a street preacher outside a football stadium, Scripture becomes downright annoying.

About a month after I moved to New York City, my new barber asked me what I did for a living.

"Wow, I've never met a religion writer," he said. "I'm still pissed off about my childhood. I was raised in the country. My parents were Southern Baptists—the hard-core fundamentalist kind. You know anything about those kinds of people?"

He had no idea that I was raised the son of an evangelical minister, a former president of the Southern Baptist Convention, and I wasn't about to disclose it.

"I mean, what do you think about all that sin and hell and judgment stuff?" he pressed.

"That's a good question."

Then I used the ultimate conversation distraction for a New Yorker: "You a Yankees or a Mets fan?"

I soon caught on to the pattern emerging in my conversations. Exchanges flowed freely when I stuck to benign topics like the dreaded winter weather or the maddening sound of jackhammers on the street. But the conversation stalled the moment the subject turned spiritual.

To avoid having to define every sacred term, I swept them into a pile and out the door. Not wanting to be associated with those in society who spoke God fluently but irresponsibly, I started avoiding spiritual conversations altogether.

I am not alone. I've been meeting people from all over, with similar histories of belief, who feel they too have been struck mute in a strange land. Terms like *sin* and *hell* have become so negative they lodge in our throats. Others, like *belief* and *salvation* have been uttered so often we don't know what they mean anymore. Definitions and connotations of words like *mercy* and *love* can no longer be assumed.

An acquaintance of mine, Kyle, is a high school pastor in the Midwest. He tells me that he struggles to motivate his students to talk about God outside of church. The issue for them, Kyle says, isn't a lack of courage. They aren't afraid of being rejected or ostracized by nonreligious friends. Rather, they lack confidence in the words they've been given. They aren't totally sure what the words mean or whether they believe they are as true as they once thought. And many in this generation have seen the hypocrisy of words not backed up by authentic actions, which causes them to pause.

Kyle's students may feel a pang of guilt for keeping quiet about sacred matters, but as it turns out, their elders are just as mute, if not more so.

Partnering with the Barna Group, a prominent social research firm focused on religion in America, I commissioned a national survey of more than 1,000 people to shine some light on this matter.[3] The survey revealed that millions of Americans—more than three-quarters of them, actually—are not speaking God often.

More than one-fifth of respondents admit they have not had a spiritual conversation *at all* in the last year.[4] Six in ten say they had a spiritual conversation only on rare occasions—either "once or twice" (29 percent) or "several times" (29 percent) in the last year. An additional 14 percent are more spiritually vocal—claiming to have had a spiritual conversation between ten and fifty times in the last year.

A paltry 7 percent of Americans say they talk about spiritual matters on about a once-per-week basis.

Here's the shocker: Despite widespread religiosity, a paltry 7 percent of Americans say they talk about spiritual matters on about a once-per-week basis (more than fifty times in the past year). That means that for most of us, our conversations almost never address the spirituality we claim as important.

That's not the only significant revelation. Political conservatives are about twice as likely as liberals to have had more than fifty conversations (10 percent versus 5 percent). More conservatives claim religious faith than do liberals, and this faith bubbles up in their conversations more often. However, liberals are still more apt to have spiritual conversations than those who claim "somewhere in between" as a political ideology—this moderate group is twice as likely as either liberals or conservatives to say they "never" have those conversations (29 percent compared to 14 percent and 16 percent, respectively). Moderates, it would seem, are more likely to keep conversations neutral, avoiding hot topics like religion and politics.

When it comes to practicing Christians who attend church regularly, I expected the frequency of spiritual conversations to skyrocket. But I was wrong, wrong, wrong. Only 13 percent of practicing Christians had a spiritual conversation more than fifty times last year, which again, would be about once per week. That means only about one in eight self-identifying Christians speak God with regular frequency.

All this may sound depressing to religious leaders and spiritual seekers, but here is the surprising silver lining: Younger generations are having *more* spiritual conversations than older generations. In fact, Millennials are having more conversations about religion or spirituality than any other generation.

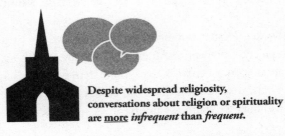

Despite widespread religiosity, conversations about religion or spirituality are <u>more</u> *infrequent* than *frequent*.

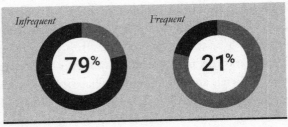

Infrequent   *Frequent*

79%   21%

n=1,019 | May 15-19, 2017

Have you had a conversation about religion or spirituality with anyone in the last year? If so, how many times?

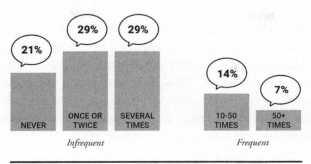

21% | NEVER

29% | ONCE OR TWICE

29% | SEVERAL TIMES

14% | 10-50 TIMES

7% | 50+ TIMES

Infrequent   *Frequent*

n=1,019 | May 15-19, 2017

The older you are, the less likely it is that you will have a spiritual conversation. Thirty-five percent of Elders say they "never" had a conversation with someone in the last year, compared to a steadily decreasing percentage from Boomers (29 percent) to Gen Xers (20 percent) to Millennials (10 percent). This trend holds true on the other end of the spectrum: Millennials are the most likely to have had between 10 and 50 conversations in the last year (18 percent compared to 11 percent of Boomers).

This renewed interest in spiritual matters among young people creates an opportunity to revive sacred speech.

Reviewing this data roused the wrangler spirit in me once more. I decided to discover why people had lost confidence in the vocabulary of faith and what, if anything, could be done to revive it. What I uncovered proved to be shocking, awakening, and transformative.

Perhaps sometimes you struggle to speak God like I did. You don't need to move to New York City, or any other urban context, to feel this tension. The world is changing from top to bottom and east to west. Our lives are now saturated with people who differ from us in race, religion, age, education, and cultural mores.

In neighborhoods across America, people don't read from the same script or work with a common spiritual vocabulary. So you may feel the pinch whether you're living in a Rocky Mountain mining town or a Great Plains farm community, in a bungalow overlooking the ocean or an HOA-friendly house in the suburbs. It doesn't matter whether you've been fluent in the vocabulary of faith since you were old enough to eat solid food or have never learned your religious ABCs.

Millions of Americans now struggle to find sacred language that can adequately describe life's deeper truths. Perhaps you've run into this awkward language barrier in recent days.

Maybe you were spoon-fed religious words since infancy but now wonder, as you've matured, whether many of those terms need to mature too.

Maybe you once believed that accepting faith meant praying certain words but now you know better.

Maybe you formerly assumed that using particular words and avoiding others somehow increased your spiritual standing.

Maybe the rigid religious tradition that you come from has made you so anxious about speaking God with precision that you end up not speaking God at all.

Maybe your parents, pastors, or friends used religious words as weapons to oppress, repress, shame, or scold you.

Maybe you've been turned off by the sharp syllables of street preachers, the slick pitches of televangelists, or the trite words of pious politicians.

Maybe you feel guilty speaking God because deep down you believe God (probably) exists on even-numbered days.

Maybe you squirm when you hear people use words to convert others, without ever considering that perhaps *they* are the ones who need converting.

Maybe you still walk into church most weeks but object to what you hear while there.

Whatever the cause of your spiritual lockjaw, I'm grateful you haven't given up. That's powerful. Because despite our frustrations, we share a common ache and desire to experience the possibility of what can happen when we're courageous enough to use the vocabulary of faith.

Ours is an expedition to rediscover a love for consecrated terms and discover why speaking God matters now more than ever. To express our spiritual stirrings, to articulate our transcendent experiences, to share our truest selves with friends. In these pages, I hope you learn to speak about faith with greater confidence than ever before.

The world needs a revival of these sacred words.

And so do we.

Let's learn to speak God from scratch.

THE LOST
LANGUAGE
OF FAITH

Does the decay of belief among educated people in the West precede the decay of language used to define and explore belief, or do we sense the fire of belief fading in us only because the words are sodden with overuse and imprecision and will not burn?

—Christian Wiman

1

Sacred Words in Crisis

Winter arrived late the year I relocated to Brooklyn, which meant I had a little extra time to enjoy New York City's autumn magic. Some days, I picked my way around my neighborhood with the goal of getting lost and striking up conversations with fascinating strangers. I once chatted with a girl who managed Barbie's social-media accounts for a living. Another day, I listened to the tales of a ninety-two-year-old woman who served as a nurse in World War II.

On chilly nights, I snuck onto my rooftop wrapped in a down comforter. Sitting under a low, dark sky, I stared for hours at the brightly lit windows of apartment buildings and commercial skyscrapers, and then concocted stories about the people I spotted.

The man sitting next to the four-foot-tall pile of file folders who hadn't gotten up from his desk in more than an hour? He lost his soul mate in a traffic accident and worked late nights to self-medicate.

The young woman thumbing through a stack of paper at her kitchen table? An associate editor at a high-powered publishing house convinced she just discovered the next Harry Potter series.

The pacing guy who seemed to be talking to himself? He was rehearsing his lines for a Broadway theater audition the next morning.

Or so I imagined.

As I settled into my big-city life, enchantment waited around every corner. I loved the way the ruby sunsets bounced off the sapphire surface of the East River. I almost fainted when I ran into my favorite *Saturday Night Live* cast member in the security line at LaGuardia Airport. Oh, and what about that time Snoop Dogg showed up to deejay at my friend's birthday party?

But the autumn magic did not linger long. Winter fell on the city like a hammer, and I was unprepared for the season's harshness. A winter coat in Georgia is an autumn jacket in New York. On far too many days, I found myself tripping through muddy snowdrifts in wet pants and soaked shoes. Most New Yorkers hibernate indoors during the frigid months, and because I hadn't made many friends yet, the coldest days were also the loneliest. Each morning I woke to yet another gray sky, the depression inched closer like a lion stalking prey.

Miserable and on the verge of admitting that my move had been a terrible mistake, I reinvested in my search for New York's magic. I ventured down to my favorite coffee shop and sat near a window, where I watched snowflakes fall. The white powder enchants even the darkest corners of the city and has the power to lift the fog of my soul.

On my darkest days, I would order a latte and an almond croissant, then unfold an old-school ink-and-paper version of the *New York Times*. (When in Rome and whatnot.) I'd flip to the opinion section, a personal favorite, where I'd search for David Brooks's latest. He wrote a column that year titled "What Our Words Tell Us," which revealed something about the language barrier that so many people of faith have encountered.[1]

Brooks constructed his argument on Google's Ngram statistics, a collection of millions of books, newspapers, and printed materials published between 1500 and 2008. This is, by far, the largest collection of literature in the history of the world. With a few keystrokes, anyone with internet access can search how frequently different words were used in literature at any point in human history. What Brooks found is that we're not speaking God as much these days as we once were.

In the Western world, religious and moral terms have significantly declined over the course of the twentieth century. One study in the *Journal of Positive Psychology* analyzed fifty terms associated with moral virtue using Google Ngram data. They discovered that a whopping 74 percent were used less frequently over the course of the last century.[2]

"Grace" . . . declined.

"Mercy" . . . declined.

"Wisdom" . . . declined.

"Faith" . . . declined.

"Sacrifice" . . . declined.

"Honesty" . . . declined.

"Righteousness" . . . declined.

"Evil" . . . declined.

One might expect meaty theological terms like *atonement* or *sanctification* to fade, but basic moral and religious words are also falling out of use.

Language about the virtues Christians call the fruit of the Spirit—words like *love, patience, gentleness,* and *faithfulness*—has become much rarer. Humility words, like *modesty,* fell by 52 percent. Compassion words, like *kindness,* dropped by 56 percent. Gratitude words, like *thankfulness,* declined by 49 percent. I don't know about you, but I miss these words and the virtues they express.

Ngram data is complicated and susceptible to misinterpretation, of course. But it suggests that our society's difficulty with speaking God is not a recent problem. This sweeping cultural shift stretches back at least a half century.

My Barna poll demonstrated that less than half of all Americans speak God regularly. But what was holding people back? I decided to take a closer look at those who speak God infrequently—only a few spiritual conversations in the last 365 days—to uncover the obstacles. When asked why they didn't have more spiritual conversations, respondents offered some surprising answers.

The most common reasons given for not engaging in conversations about religion and spirituality appear to fall into three broad categories: indifference, ignorance, and avoidance.

The most common reasons given for not engaging in spiritual conversations fall into three broad categories:

Ignorance vs. Indifference vs. Avoidance

Ignorance
17%

Indifference
23%

Avoidance
63%

Note: Asked only of those who speak God infrequently. Respondents could select any that applied.

n=508 | May 15-19, 2017

Nearly a quarter of respondents said, "I'm not religious and I don't care about these kinds of topics" (23 percent). Much ink has been spilled by cultural commentators explaining why fewer Americans are affiliating with religion these days—they feel religion is often judgmental, hypo-critical, unwelcoming of doubts, oppressive to women, opposed to sci-ence. Regardless of their motivations, they are apathetic about religious language because religion itself is unimportant to them. And people don't talk about what they don't care about.

Do any of the following express why you do not have spiritual conversations more often?

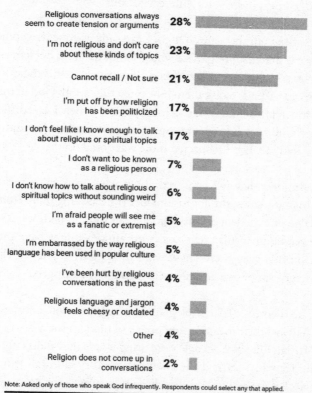

Religious conversations always seem to create tension or arguments	28%
I'm not religious and don't care about these kinds of topics	23%
Cannot recall / Not sure	21%
I'm put off by how religion has been politicized	17%
I don't feel like I know enough to talk about religious or spiritual topics	17%
I don't want to be known as a religious person	7%
I don't know how to talk about religious or spiritual topics without sounding weird	6%
I'm afraid people will see me as a fanatic or extremist	5%
I'm embarrassed by the way religious language has been used in popular culture	5%
I've been hurt by religious conversations in the past	4%
Religious language and jargon feels cheesy or outdated	4%
Other	4%
Religion does not come up in conversations	2%

Note: Asked only of those who speak God infrequently. Respondents could select any that applied.

n=508 | May 15-19, 2017

Indifference to sacred speech has a built-in positive feedback mechanism. As people become more apathetic about religious conversations, the topic of spirituality comes up less frequently. People are less apt to identify spiritual forces at work or wonder about a "higher being" or even discuss morality. Unless something is done to stoke interest in spiritual matters, apathy will become a driving force in the death spiral of spiritual speech.

In addition to lack of interest, some people avoid religious and spiritual conversations due to a lack of information. Seventeen percent of respondents said, "I don't feel like I know enough to talk about religious or spiritual topics." This answer implies a level of ignorance—that is, a lack of knowledge or exposure—for different reasons.

Given that the numbers are so high, I can only assume that some of the ignorance is shared among those who grew up religious but left, as well as those who still practice today. When I first received this data, I phoned my *Christian* friends to ask them how often they speak God in their daily lives. Most replied "rarely" or "almost never." When I asked them why not, they said they didn't know. Spiritual conversations just didn't come up, they told me. But I suspected more was going on.

Some admitted they felt confused about what spiritual words actually mean. In many cases, the confusion doesn't necessarily result from lack of knowledge or experience with speaking of God. Sometimes, it's the opposite. People in insular religious communities might have used some words so often they don't know what they mean anymore. The words have become shopworn and now slip through their fingers.

Before he died in 2015, theologian Marcus Borg noted that Christian words had lost their meaning and power in modern society—in part due to "Christian illiteracy." People were using words they didn't understand, he said. They had learned the twentieth-century cultural definitions of Christian language, but they had little exposure to the centuries of history behind these words.

"The problem is not simply unfamiliarity," Borg wrote. "Many of us have heard Christian language since childhood. If we are still part of the church, we continue to hear it in biblical readings, sermons, hymns, prayers, liturgies, and creeds. We are steeped in it."[3]

Part of the problem in American society is the proliferation of *Christianese,* a term that refers to the common slang used inside Christian communities. These words do not always translate well in secular spaces or make sense to those from other religious traditions. Which means, ironically, that the word *Christianese* can itself be classified as Christianese.

Sometimes this term is assigned to sacred terms used by Christians throughout the centuries—*sin, salvation, baptism, the blood of the Lamb.* But most often the label is attributed to weird phrases that are unique to modern forms of Christianity but rarely or never appear in sacred texts or Church history.

Have you ever given a "love offering" or started a "prayer chain"? Have you asked God for "traveling mercies" or a "hedge of protection"? Do you ever talk about "doing life together" or "seeing the fruit" of someone's life? Have you ever had a "quiet time" or confronted someone with "truth in love" or labeled someone a "backslider"? If so, then you may be fluent in Christianese.

The reasons for disliking Christianese are legion and many are legitimate. These words and phrases give the appearance of authentic spirituality while fostering the opposite. Clichés, Christian or not, are unable to convey the true heart of an individual's story.

Christianese can also draw a troubling line between "insiders" and "outsiders." In his book *Folkways: A Study of the Sociological Importance of Usages, Manners, Customs, Mores, and Morals,* William Graham Sumner demonstrated that as communal habits and customs (like the use of Christianese) form over time, an in-group develops favoritism toward other insiders and heaps contempt on outsiders.[4] In this way, Christianese can nurture unhealthy perspectives among its speakers and create an unnecessary chasm for nonspeakers.

It's not just the strangeness of Christianese, but its familiarity, that is problematic.

I asked my friend Kathy what she meant when she said, "I asked Jesus into my heart." Where did the image of Jesus entering an artery and aorta come from, and what was she trying to express exactly? Kathy paused in confusion—she had never been asked that before. Finally, she said this phrase meant she's "saved." What did the word *saved* mean, I asked her?

Kathy looked confused for a moment. "Saved," she explained, meant she'd accepted God's "gift of grace." But what does that "gift" mean, I pressed. Exasperated, she circled back, "It means that I asked Jesus into my heart!"

My questions didn't invalidate my friend's sincere belief system. But many people—even devout believers who speak God with apparent ease—define religious words using religious words. A series of questions about what they mean leads back to where the discussion began.

No wonder spiritual language can feel so awkward.

Most people's lives teach them that language—whether sung or spoken—is important. The words we choose and the way we use them matters. But we do not often quiet ourselves long enough to ask, *What am I saying when I'm saying what I'm saying?*

In addition to indifference and ignorance, many respondents said they shrink back and avoid spiritual conversations for various reasons. Some said speaking God always seems to create tension or arguments (28 percent), while others feel put off by how religion has been politicized (17 percent). In this tense cultural climate, you've probably encountered social conflict due to talking about religion or politics or some combination of the two.

Others still report not wanting to appear religious (7 percent), sound weird (6 percent), or seem extreme (5 percent). Maybe you had a neighbor stop talking to you because she was put off by your religiosity, or perhaps a coworker avoids you because he is afraid you're going to douse him with spiritual-speak.

In total, a whopping 63 percent of respondents fell into the avoidance category, saying they steered clear of such dialogue, albeit for various reasons.

Even a lifelong God-speaker like me can empathize with the reasons some people avoid spiritual conversations.

THE POLITICIZATION OF SACRED WORDS

For every American who is reticent to speak God, there is an American politician with the opposite problem. Sacred language has been politicized, which is why many people say they are abandoning it.

Turn on your television in any election season, and you'll likely hear a candidate speaking God. The ubiquity of religious language in political speeches is an American tradition, but the way these words are twisted for partisan ends can leave you holding clumps of your own hair.

During election years, political hopefuls make appearances at influential churches, often offering invocations or even preaching sermons. On the campaign trail, politicians co-opt the vocabulary of faith to attract religious voting blocs. Their words may seem harmless or coincidental, but many point out that these appeals are often used as dog whistles that the faithful respond to.[5]

In 1999, when I was a senior in high school, George W. Bush released a book as he made his bid for the presidency called *A Charge to Keep: My Journey to the White House*. To the nonreligious ear, the title may sound poetic, perhaps innocuous, but its meaning is clear. Drawn from the Charles Wesley hymn "A Charge to Keep I Have," in which the first stanza reads,

> A charge to keep I have,
> A God to glorify,
> A never-dying soul to save,
> And fit it for the sky.

Neither the hymn nor its themes are the subject of Bush's book. But the title proved recognizable to many Christians. Before I flipped to the first page, I felt like this George Bush guy must be "one of us."[6]

President Bush continued to use religious language and hymnology regularly while he was in office. In his 2003 State of the Union speech, he identified "wonder-working power" in the values of the American people. The secular audience might have appreciated the alliteration but little more. Yet many Christians recognized the famous hymn, which declares there's "wonder-working power" in the blood of Jesus.

Donald Trump carried on the tradition of becoming more outwardly religious when running for office. Because of his well-documented personal history, his attempts have been more noticeable and more awkward than those of his predecessors. The real estate mogul–turned-politician confessed he's never actually asked God for forgiveness. Even his church denied he was an active member. Yet Trump played the Christian card with impunity. He waved his Bible at a voter rally and accused the IRS of auditing him because of his religion. On his first National Day of Prayer, Trump stumbled through a religious speech and jokingly asked the nation to pray for Arnold Schwarzenegger's low ratings on *The Apprentice.*

From Ronald Reagan and both Bushes to Bill Clinton and Barack Obama, presidents of both major parties have used sacred language with the seeming intent to manipulate and mobilize the electorate. This is an American political tradition. But when high-profile politicians speak God in the most perfunctory manner possible, it's no wonder supporters and opponents alike avoid speaking God altogether. Many Americans are put off by the way the vocabulary of faith has been manipulated for political ends.

THE EXPLOITATION OF SACRED WORDS

Religious leaders who mishandle or misuse sacred words can deeply damage people's lives.

Consider Danielle Campoamor. After being physically abused by her husband, her pastor told her that she just needed to "pray more." She started to realize that trusted church leaders had used sacred language to control her family. Words that hurt Danielle over the years included being labeled as a "doubter" (an epithet in her community) and a "nonbeliever" (even worse). When she asked questions about her faith, she was accused of "missing the point."

Danielle quit religion altogether and concluded, "the Christian faith has failed to lead by example. It's failed to stand for its principles. By positing itself and its followers as the purveyors of the moral high ground, it's allowed cowardice in the face of blatant immorality. It happened when my pastor came face to face with an abused woman. It happened when a Christian friend called me a murderer after I had an abortion at 23. It happens now, today."[7]

Danielle's story is not just about the abuse of power. It is about relation-ships broken and trust severed and losing a faith that was once a source of life. Her story is one that too many share.

Have you ever had a person of authority use sacred words as a weapon of guilt and shame against you? Know anyone who uses religious language to police others' personal life choices or judge those who don't adhere to their ethical standards?

I have friends who say that the most "loving" thing they can do is tell their "lost" friends that they are going to hell. The use of their words de-fines a meaning I cannot accept. *Love* is drained of compassion and forged into a machete, and *Lost* no longer describes the inability of *all* humans to find our way forward on our own. Their words separate a lesser *them* from a better *us*.

Growing up, I obsessed over how my eternal future hung in the balance. My church taught that saying a particular prayer would defeat my inner demons and earn me a golden ticket to heaven. But these types of churches also make congregants question whether they really, really mean these prayers. (Apparently, prayers don't stick if you don't mean them enough.)

The result was repeated conversions, which looked good on the church's annual salvation reports. But it meant that many congregants like me often woke from nightmares about burning in hell and prayed to ask Jesus into their hearts yet again—just in case it didn't work the last time.

Tracing this fear back to its origin is tricky, but the best I can tell, it started after my church put on a theater production with the warm-and-welcoming title *Heaven's Gates and Hell's Flames*. As the name suggests, the touring theater production tells stories of people dying and finding themselves at a crossroads between heaven and hell.

If the actor who got hit by a car happened to pray one of those prayers (and really meant it), then he was welcomed into heaven. The audience sighed in collective relief. Maybe even cheered, depending on your church. But if the actor had never been converted, demons would emerge wearing masks like the murderer from the *Scream* films. The actor would begin screaming and begging and pleading for his life as the demons dragged him off to hell. At this, fear and doubt swept across even the most pious audience members.

While many churches have no interest in this particular type of production, untold thousands of them make us suspicious of these kinds of tactics. Whether the afterlife works as portrayed in *Heaven's Gates and Hell's Flames* is debatable, but of serious concern is the way many churches have used words to induce terror and prompt an emotional response.

To hear them tell of it . . .

- "God" is a nearly heartless monster who almost relishes punishing people.
- "Faith" is an insurance policy that provides postmortem fire protection. Just sign on the dotted line. (And really mean it.)
- "Conversion" is a decision driven mostly by fear. Joy is ancillary.
- "Grace" is more rational than beautiful.
- "Mystery" is, well, not part of the equation.

People who have spent time in church communities like this often end up reevaluating these assumptions later in life. Since the definitions of these terms are deeply embedded in those religious communities themselves, some choose to walk away from religion altogether.

According to a recent study, young people often leave the church because of the judgmental, simplistic, exclusivist teachings of churches that are unfriendly to matters like doubt.[8] And as the data shows, when they leave the community of faith, they often abandon the vocabulary of faith too.

THE POLARIZATION OF SACRED WORDS

In an increasingly pluralistic, and in some cases secularizing, society, some people fear what others might think if they speak about spiritual matters. As the saying goes, it's impolite to talk about politics and religion in mixed company. Some fear that breaking these social rules might make them appear to be religious fanatics.

Public schools are a microcosm of where speaking words of faith are complicated. The US Department of Education grants public-school students the right to express their faith in conversations with classmates, by reading their Bibles at school, praying in public, and even by inserting their beliefs into assignments. But some claim the rules are not followed consistently in all districts.

A teacher in Shelby County, Tennessee, for example, told ten-year-old Erin Shead that she was prohibited from writing about God as her "hero." The child then wrote two papers—one about God and another about Michael Jackson. The former was rejected.[9] Shead's paper about God was eventually accepted with legal help from a religious-liberty litigation firm.[10] If you have to sue the school to be able to speak about your faith, you can imagine how it might subtly form one's perspective about God-speak. When sacred rhetoric feels socially risky, no wonder some people are afraid to do it at all.

Millennials are much more likely to feel afraid that people will see them as a fanatic or extremist: 10 percent compared to 4 percent of Boomers. Young people have grown up in a culture that values tolerance and giving people the freedom to make their own decisions.[11]

Additionally, Millennials are more likely than any other age group to have friends who are different from them—different ethnicities, different religions, different social and political beliefs. Therefore, they are likely more sensitive to coming across as judgmental toward those groups. Millennials hope to build a more pluralistic society and therefore fear being associated with a group that is often represented as being opposed to other ways of thinking or believing. According to another study by the Barna Group, a majority of Americans now believe it is "extreme" to "attempt to convert others" to your faith.[12]

Who wants to be seen as extremist or fanatic or a pushy proselytizer? If speaking God could cause social backlash, many Americans conclude that perhaps it's safer not to speak God at all.

As winter waned in New York City, I hibernated at home, plowing my way through a stack of films while the snow melted. One of my favorites was *No Country for Old Men,* adapted from the novel by Cormac McCarthy. In the movie's haunting final scene, the laconic lawman Sheriff Bell recounts a dream he's been having.

A horse galloped into the cold and into the night. Atop the steed sat a blanket-wrapped man, face downturned and silence on his lips. In the man's hand was an animal's horn. The keratin shell glowed like the moon from the blazing embers inside. The man raced with determination, as if nothing else in the world mattered or even existed. He had to make it to the nearest camp and pass on the fire before the embers died out.

McCarthy fans and book critics alike have long debated the meaning of fire in the film. Many believe it symbolizes yesteryear or older ways of life. The tradition of carrying fire from one town to the next was passed down to the pioneers from the Native Americans. But this tradition had long since passed away by the time Sheriff Bell dreams it. So this is Bell's realization that he now lives in "no country for old men" and that his deceased father has taken the fire ahead to meet him on the other side of death.[13]

But we might also imagine the fire in McCarthy's horn to be a metaphor for language—specifically sacred language. Words are the fires we carry to each other, but the embers do not originate with us. They were handed to us by messengers from generations past, and now we pass them on to others.

When we lose our spiritual vocabulary, we lose much more than words. We lose the power of speaking grace, forgiveness, love, and justice over others.

One of my heroes is a seminary student named Jonathan Myrick Daniels. In March 1965, he encountered a fire-starter named Martin Luther King Jr., who spoke of "injustice" and "equality" and "hope"; the words sparked like struck flint off King's speech and landed in the student's heart. King called for volunteers to come to Selma, Alabama, to secure voting rights for black Americans, and Daniels felt compelled to go.

Something in Selma blew across the embers Daniels had received from King, and a fire flickered. Taking a leave of absence from seminary, Daniels joined the Civil Rights protests rippling across the South. He protested racist businesses that participated in price gouging, the quality of education for black students, and discriminatory hiring practices. The modest campfire was a blazing bonfire now.

"Sometimes we take to the streets, sometimes we yawn through interminable meetings. . . . Sometimes we confront the posse, sometimes we hold a child," Daniels later described his work.[14]

In August of 1965, little more than a week after President Lyndon Johnson signed the Voting Rights Act, Daniels joined thirty people in rural

Alabama to protest local business owners' unequal treatment of black customers. He and the others were arrested and transferred to the county seat in a garbage truck.

Daniels spent six days in a sweltering cell with no air-conditioning and, reportedly, no showers or toilets. When morale among prisoners fell, Daniels led group prayers and sang hymns. His fire would not be extinguished so easily.

Upon release, he and some of his fellow demonstrators tried to purchase a soda at a nearby store. But when seventeen-year-old Ruby Sales, one of two black demonstrators with Daniels, stepped up to enter the store, a county special deputy with a 12-gauge shotgun stepped out. A gust of wind, a fanned flame, and Daniels pulled the girl aside and stepped in front. Two shotgun blasts, and Daniels was dead.

The deputy was tried for manslaughter, not murder. An all-white jury acquitted him and then, one by one, shook his hand as he left the courthouse.[15] With this verdict, the embers that King passed to Daniels were picked up by horns around the country and carried from town to town.

The Episcopal Church named Daniels a martyr and gave him an official feast day on their calendar, alongside the likes of Dietrich Bonhoeffer. Decades after his death, Daniels's words and actions still warm our lives.

Stories of people like Daniels illustrate how spiritual language ignites a fire that grows into transformative power and goodness. We don't always recognize all the fire-carriers who illuminate our lives. Perhaps they are long-dead authors or preachers or activists whose stories have meant more to people than they'll ever know. These embers glowed in our lives without our noticing.

The process is not foolproof and only works as long as someone is willing to carry it forward. If we fail to stoke the flames, they will snuff out. And if we misuse them, the flames rage and people run for their lives. As with real fire, it can either heat our homes or burn them to the ground. In our current age, it seems, the fire of sacred speech is fading due to indifference and ignorance and avoidance. Bonfires have become campfires, campfires have become embers, and embers have become ashes.

Sacred speech is in crisis as millions of fire-carriers have decided to extinguish their torches. But a lingering question remains unanswered: *So what?* Why does it matter if we speak God anyway?

2

Why Speaking God Matters

Anyone wanting to learn about our society's changing relationship with words must only visit a library. America has more of them than one might expect—an estimated 119,487—but that number is declining.

Federal library funding has dropped nearly 40 percent since 2000, and the resources for physical libraries are evaporating, which leaves me grieving. These book banks provided more childhood memories than I can count on my fingers and toes. Thumbing through the hand-typed card catalogs at my elementary school library felt like rummaging through travel brochures to exotic lands.

Should I trek to Idaville to solve mysteries with Encyclopedia Brown today or enroll in Crunchem Hall Primary School alongside Matilda Wormwood?

The gloom I feel about the disappearance of libraries transcends nostalgia. Libraries hold more than books—they also contain salvation. Inside the maze of shelves or nestled into a reading room, we are saved from life's frenetic pace. Rescued from the illusion that every thought worth thinking can be boiled down to 280 characters or a handful of hashtags. Saved from a world in which the only words we encounter are the ones trending.

Fewer people are utilizing these places of solace. A recent Pew Research poll reported that 65 percent of American adults believe closing their public library would have a major impact on their community, but only

32 percent say their closure would have a major effect on them or their families. Less than half of Americans have visited a library in the past twelve months.[1] As a writer and reader, this rends my heart.

The digital age has eliminated the need for many items that were once indispensible—landlines, cameras, wristwatches, even cash registers. And when was the last time you saw, much less used, a telephone booth? To avoid a similar fate, libraries are reinventing themselves and becoming job placement centers, computer labs, gaming portals, and Wi-Fi hubs that attract freelancers in a gig economy.[2]

Some fear that this conversion will mark a change in how humans encounter words, at least in long form. The first *all-digital* library opened to the public in San Antonio, Texas, in 2013, after all. Bookless libraries were once an oxymoron, but now many believe they are unavoidable. Would such a shift redefine our society's relationship with words, solidifying our preference for bite-sized ideas or Instagram visuals, packaged for digital consumption?

I wondered this as I climbed the steps of the historic New York Public Library. Two marble lion statues grace the entrance, nicknamed Lady Astor and Lord Lenox after the library's founders. In the 1930s, Mayor LaGuardia renamed them Patience and Fortitude after two virtues he felt New Yorkers needed to endure the Great Depression. Their more recent titles stuck, perhaps since visitors need a double portion of patience and fortitude to investigate the more than one hundred miles of bookshelves inside.

This particular library is known for more than its books. Stowed in safe-keeping are special items closed to the public—a 1493 letter from Christopher Columbus announcing his discovery of the New World, Truman Capote's cigar case, and locks of hair from famed writers Charlotte Bronte and Walt Whitman, as well as Wild Bill Hickok.

But I'm not looking for any historical figures' tresses today. No, I've come to explore the history of dead languages.

Although religious speech may not be a language in a formal sense, it functions like one. Three of the most fundamental components of a language include:

- **Vocabulary**: A set of words unique to a particular community that is spoken and/or appears in written form.
- **Grammar**: A set of rules, either formalized or understood, that help govern how the vocabulary should be used.
- **Community**: A group of people who feel a sense of solidarity by using the vocabulary.[3]

Since speaking God meets these requirements, I wondered whether the history of dead languages held the key to understanding the difficulties facing sacred language. If the vocabulary of faith is fading, I wanted to know why and what, if anything, should be done to stop it.

I sat cross-legged in an aisle with piles of books stacked around me like campfire kindling. Sifting through these volumes reminded me that there are so many words I will never know. Each time I encountered an unfamiliar string of letters—*calque, mumpsimus, acrolect*—I Googled the definition on my smartphone. Who knew that *illeism* refers to a tendency to refer to oneself in the third person? Or that *cryptophasia* describes a secret language only understood by twins, developed as they age?

Overwhelmed by so many peculiar phrases, I decided to focus on scanning basic texts to learn the fundamentals on which scholars agree. Linguists, like pastors and politicians, don't agree on much. They differ over when a child's language-acquisition window closes. They debate whether learning language is an innate human skill or an acquired one. They disagree on how to categorize a new language. *Do emojis count?* But they all agree that, well—words matter.

A month after we are born, our ears open to the swirling world of words. As infants, we notice the shapes of mouths and the way syllables are formed. Our baby bodies respond by cooing and smiling and kicking. These behaviors can make adults cheer and applaud like sea lions, but they are actually physiological indicators that children are learning to listen. For months, this process builds until the magic moment when we begin to speak words of our own—usually "Da-da" or "hi" or "uh-oh" or, in my case, "NO!"

> Syllables and sentences are a powerful arsenal with the potential to do much good or evil, depending on how they are used.

All of us, except those born deaf, have passed through this process from learning to listen to learning to speak. And, mostly unnoticed, it is always happening all around us. But it doesn't take us long to realize that syllables and sentences, phrases and clauses, are a powerful arsenal with the potential to do much good or evil, depending on how they are used.

I don't remember the first time I realized the power of words, but I will never forget the first time I noticed it. My sophomore year of high school I transferred to a new school across town and was forced to start rebuilding my social life from the ground up. At the time, I was a geeky kid with a goofy haircut and no discernable sense of style. In high school, this combination makes one both insecure and a target for cruel kids.

Bill was a bully. Plain and simple. Those who crossed him were made to regret their hubris, and as a senior, he demanded the respect and fear of almost every other student. To this day, I don't know what I did to deserve his ire. I cannot remember ever speaking to him or anyone in his immediate circle of influence.

As I opened my locker and bent down to retrieve my TI-85 supercalculator, Bill glanced in my direction and uttered six letters that hit me like a shotgun shell: "Faggot." The whole hall seemed to slow as students' heads turned to glimpse Bill's latest prey. Then came the snickers. Crude gestures. Brutal laughter. I headed to class with an emotional limp.

Bill's words were not a statement about my sexuality. They were a knee-jerk comment on my otherness and my gawkiness. But the result was the same. Over the next several weeks, Bill labeled me with that awful epithet until my parents engaged the administration. The bullying stopped; the damage remained. My limp had become a chronic condition.

I was now the school leper. Unclean and untouchable. Perhaps other students feared that any contact might spark Bill's wrath toward them. Or maybe I perceived more rejection than I actually received. Either way, I languished in loneliness until Heather stepped in. Also a senior, she took me under her wing and introduced me to kindhearted people. She sat with me at lunch, which had become the most isolating and humiliating part of my day.

"Why are you being so nice to me?" I finally asked.

"Because I am your . . . friend," Heather replied.

In a moment, those words broke over me and mended my wounds. I had a . . . *friend*. An actual, breathing friend who liked me for me, who wasn't embarrassed to acknowledge my existence, and who was willing to stand by me even if others would not.

Those two words beginning with the same consonant, both six-letters in length, were powerful enough to both harm and heal. They shared significant, soul-shaping effects, albeit in opposite directions. They were two sides of the same coin. One was a bomb, the other a balm. And so it is with all the words we speak. They can raise up or tear down, spur forward or tether back.

If asked to recall a time when words caused emotional impact in your life, I suspect you wouldn't need to think long. You might mention a parent's consoling words after a painful disappointment or the sadistic words of a classmate. Maybe you think of the last words your child shouted before disappearing from your life. Or the phrase a friend whispered the day after your mother passed away.

Words impact our emotions and influence the paths we pursue. "I love you" spoken by the right person at the right moment will set your heart ablaze. "I'm leaving you" can incinerate you into an ash pile. A baby muttering "Ma-ma" can soften an anxious mother, while a toddler shouting "Help!" can panic a father. A teacher's decision to say "Yes, you can" as opposed to "You'll never succeed" can determine whether a student grows up into a sculptor or a scientist. A simple "I'm sorry" can mend what's broken.

Whoever created the famous line about sticks and stones must never have been bullied. In our most vulnerable moments, the words spoken to us, about us, and over us can pulverize our souls until we drown in tears. Words can snap a human in two without spilling blood. This makes them at least as powerful—and dangerous—as either sticks or stones. All with a beating heart know this to be true.

Entering the world of linguistics revealed that words' power reaches far beyond our emotions. An emerging body of research now reveals that the languages we hear and speak influence our worldviews, memories, perceptions, and behaviors more than scientists once realized. Children who grow up speaking the same language tend to think in similar ways.[4] Our words shape our minds.

A linguist named Lera Boroditsky once asked an audience of celebrated scholars at Harvard University to close their eyes and point north. Hands shot up around the auditorium like roman candles, aimed in all possible directions. She repeated the experiment at Princeton and Stanford, as well as in Moscow, London, and Beijing. The result was always the same—an array of hands aimed at each of the four major directions and every point in between.

But when Boroditsky traveled to a community on the western shores of Australia's Cape York, she discovered that children as young as five can point north at all times with absolute precision.

Why the difference? The answer, as it turns out, is words.

Many languages in the Western world use relative spatial terms. At an amusement park, you might complain that a stranger cut in "front" of you and ask them to step "behind" you. Or when unpacking boxes, you might ask someone to place your alarm clock on the "left" end table or the "right" one.

Language influences our worldviews, memories, perceptions, and behaviors more than scientists once realized.

But the Aboriginal language spoken in that region of Australia—along with a third of the world's languages—use cardinal directions, which direct toward the four points on a compass, to discuss space. Someone speaking one of these languages might say something like, "My knife is southeast of my plate" or "Jackie is standing to the north of Trisha."[5] Because of their language, they are always aware of the sun's position in the sky and develop an awareness of their changing orientation as they navigate their surroundings.

"As a result of this constant linguistic training," Boroditsky writes, "speakers of such languages are remarkably good at staying oriented and keeping track of where they are, even in unfamiliar landscapes."[6]

If you talk about north, you think about north. If you don't, you won't.

Language's influence doesn't end with perceptions of direction.[7] Words shape the way we view the world, including our sense of morality. Linguistic studies show that when an altercation occurs, speakers of some languages are more likely to assign blame than others. In English, we prefer active verb constructions ("Sarah wrecked the car") instead of passive ("The car was wrecked"). If someone asks you to recount an event or recall a memory, your language conditions you to assign agency, even if an action was accidental. But if you speak a language like Japanese or Spanish, the agent of causality is usually dropped, even if someone was at fault.

If a friend goes on a liquor-fueled bender and wraps your Honda around an oak tree, someone who speaks Japanese or Spanish might say, "The car was wrecked."[8] As a result, people who speak languages like English more readily blame others and have developed a "criminal-justice bent toward punishing transgressors rather than restituting victims."[9]

Since words influence our *whichaway, whatsit,* and *whodunit,* you won't be surprised to learn that they also affect our self-perceptions.

Hebrew is one of the many languages that assign genders to nouns. If a Hebrew speaker declares that she will make a "list" in a "notebook," for example, she must use two feminine nouns. Someone in a Finnish-speaking culture, however, uses words with no gender markings. (English falls somewhere between these two.)

What difference does this make? Hebrew-speaking children become aware of their own gender a full year earlier than kids who speak Finnish. (English-speaking children fall somewhere in between the two groups.)[10]

Words also shape behavior patterns. For example, English is a language that distinguishes between the past, present, and future when speaking of time. Chinese does not—speakers use the same words when talking about an event that happened yesterday or one that will happen tomorrow. As a result, they make different economic decisions than do Westerners.

People groups who speak more about *now* than *in the future* think more about today than tomorrow. They are more likely to spend their money, smoke, and practice unsafe sex. The data indicates that if a person speaks about the future as a time distinct from the present, he will perceive it as more distant and less pressing.[11]

Both speakers and listeners are transformed by these strings of letters we call words. They influence what we pay attention to and how we see others and ourselves. Think about it: two people speaking two different languages will describe a single event in distinct, often incompatible ways.[12]

Words even influence our experiences of the world and which mental images stick in our minds.

"Every word is a window," writes Gregory Spencer, professor of communication at Westmont College.[13] From the moment our infant ears open to the world, the words and phrases flooding in begin to shape us. Our ears, eyes, and mouths are entwined. That is, the language we *speak* and *hear* forms the lens through which we *see* the world. Speaking shapes societies because words whittle worldviews.

My time at the New York Public Library was now coming to a close. Uncovering the hidden powers of language left me feeling even more unnerved about the decline in sacred speech. If we do not use sacred words, then our minds will be less attuned to transcendence. If we do not have spiritual conversations, then we'll be less shaped by our spirituality. And if moral language is vanishing—with the decline of words like *grace, mercy, honest, courage,* and *wisdom*—then we can expect our communities and culture will reflect this shift.

Well-chosen words empower us to express compassion and extend kindness. They equip us to bring out the best in others and ourselves. They help us extend grace when we feel stingy and offer hope when all appears dim. They help us cross the threshold from how the world is to how it ought to be.

Speaking God matters because speaking *always* matters.

3

Our Divine Linguaphile

After I searched the library stacks and scavenged the internet, I returned to a piece of literature I felt I needed to consult once more. I retrieved a well-worn, leather-bound volume from atop my bookshelf and settled into a chair in the great reading room to spend time devouring the pages of the Bible. As it turns out, God is something of a linguaphile too.[1]

In the poetry of the first chapter of Genesis, God creates the world with words. God uses language to form seaweed and sunflowers, caterpillars and cats, riptides and meteors. But God doesn't stop there. With a whisper, humans arise from dirt and divine breath inflates lungs.

At this point, the story goes, the Creator gave humans a gift: the *imago dei,* or image of God. For centuries theologians have debated what this "image" consists of. Some say it's intellect, others claim it is the ability to reason, and others still contend that it is the ability to obey a moral code. Another possibility is that the *imago dei* is our ability to speak. After all, God's first command to humans is to formulate a vocabulary by assigning names to animals and objects.

Communicating with words is a unique part of what makes us human. Have you ever wondered why *Homo sapiens* speak, but plants, insects, and even other animals do not? Sure, some creatures communicate with motion and sound. Bees can *bzzzz* their location, seals can honk to signal their delight, and I sometimes think that my family's Boston terrier barks in full sentences. But no animal can relay the texture, nuance, color, and emotion that we humans do with our words.[2]

Language is so unique to our species that it threatened to capsize Charles Darwin's theory of natural selection from the get-go. When he first published *The Origin of Species* in 1859, the evidence he presented rattled the world. But linguists and other scholars soon pointed out that language could not be explained by natural selection. The power of language transcends the need for survival, and the components of the human brain required for it are too complex and advanced to have developed over time. The ability to speak sets apart humans from animals at such a gaping distance from each other that Darwin's hypothesis cannot come close to explaining how the evolution of language could have happened.

Alfred Wallace, a friend of Darwin's who may have been the first to actually articulate evolutionary theory, noted that the brain's ability to reason and speak was so advanced beyond the needs of human survival that natural selection was inadequate to account for it. While evolutionary progression may explain earth's many species, Wallace concluded that the emergence of complex speech required intervention from a supernatural power or superior intelligence.[3]

More than 150 years after Darwin's theory debuted, our best minds have still not been able to show how language could have arisen through natural selection. In 2014, a group of premier evolutionists, anthropologists, and linguists (including famed linguist Noam Chomsky himself) released a peer-reviewed article titled "The Mystery of Language Evolution." Despite robust efforts to explain how language emerged, they concluded, "The most fundamental questions about the origins and evolution of our linguistic capacity remain as mysterious as ever."[4]

Language is the greatest tool possessed by any creature. No other animals besides humans have ever possessed this capability—and none ever will.

As Reynolds Price writes in *A Palpable God,* the ability to speak and tell stories is essential to our species—"second in necessity apparently after nourishment and before love and shelter."[5] Many in cities around the world survive without homes or hugs, but almost none live in silence. You might call us *Homo verba*. We are word-shaped beings who live word-shaped lives within word-shaped communities.

This, it seems, is by design.

As one Episcopal writer says, "God could have made us stone creatures, tree creatures, sea creatures, winged creatures, but God made us speech creatures instead. Human beings made in God's own likeness, which is to say, capable of joining God in the work of creation by speaking things into being ourselves."[6]

> **We are word-shaped beings who live word-shaped lives within word-shaped communities. This, it seems, is by design.**

Words are one of God's holy gifts to humanity, and speaking them should be a sacred act. We drape our dreams in words; we paint murals of sorrows with them. They are humanity's carrier pigeons of information, of meaning, of emotion. We struggle to live without them.

But we humans don't always wield our words well. We often speak without much thought. We spew hate speech and blaspheme, transforming the sacred act of speaking into profane behavior. We speak deceptively and unkindly. We use words to curse, tear down, discourage, blame, and judge. A simple *no* can fly from our lips with the decimating power of a shotgun shell, while a sincere *yes* can alter the course of a life.

As a writer, I depend on words. I know how much they matter. The words I choose to include in a column or book can encourage the discouraged, irk the easily irritated, or educate the uninformed. There are a million ways to discuss any particular topic; the choice and the arrangement of words always matter.

What is true of me is also true of us all.

Our words may not cause plants to sprout, but they can make hope spring forth in a human heart. God birthed us with words, and now we find ourselves in constant labor, giving birth ourselves through the power of words. When we release words into the air, like the first ones spoken, they create worlds both glorious and dark.

———————

The notion that sacred words are powerful and essential saturates both the Jewish and Christian traditions. When Moses descended Mount Sinai lugging two stone tablets, he was delivering ten sentences that would become Israel's watchwords. The commandments make for a curious list, really. One addresses the need for rest, and another forbids cheating on your spouse. Stealing is out in one commandment, while another vetoes covetousness. Idol-making is off-limits, and children are ordered to honor their parents.

But when it comes to words, God issued not one, but two commandments. One prohibits bearing false witness against another person, which is just a fancy way of saying that hate speech, slander, and lying are all bad news. Another commandment forbids people from taking God's name in vain. Words are too powerful to use carelessly, especially when you're speaking God.

Years after Moses chiseled the Decalogue, words continued to play a prominent role. In the Jewish tradition, stories were passed between generations around campfires long before the inventions of pens, parchment, or even papyrus. Ancient Israel was, in the phrasing of theologian Walter Brueggemann, "primarily a community of utterance."[7] Jewish leaders and prophets were deemed faithful or condemned by the words they spoke or withheld.

Twentieth-century French philosopher Helene Cixous remarked, "It is said that life and death are under the power of language." But an ancient Hebrew king named Solomon actually beat her to the punch by a couple thousand years: "The tongue has the power of life and death, and those who love it will eat its fruit."[8] A thoughtless word, the wise monarch said, is like the fatal thrust of a sword, while a phrase wrapped in love is medicine.[9]

Perhaps none of the ancient Jews knew more about linguistic power than Solomon's father, David. When he was a boy and still smelled of musty lamb's wool, a prophet spoke words over him about his destiny as king. When a giant threatened his nation, he spoke defiant words in defense of his people and then slayed that giant with stones from a shepherd's bag.

When David gave up herding sheep for ruling a nation, he took up a different kind of stone. Through his psalms, the shepherd-turned-king used words to vent and lament, bless and praise. The psalms spanned generations as Jews recited, sung, and prayed them. Hundreds of years after David's body was laid to rest, his words still proved powerful enough to slay the giants of depression and discouragement and bitterness and loss.

Christianity inherited these ideas from its Jewish mother and drew them forward. Jesus launched his ministry in his hometown synagogue, announcing that he had been anointed by God to *proclaim*—that is, to speak God—and the last three years of Jesus' life were "first and foremost a ministry of words."[10] He would say "Come, follow me" and "Your faith has healed you" and "Go and sin no more" and "Blessed are the meek." With each proclamation, closed doors swung wide and lame legs danced and blind eyes could see.

Jesus loved language so much that he often delivered odes to linguistics.[11] He said good people should utter life-giving language, that we will have to justify the way we speak in the afterlife, and that humans can't live by bread alone but by nourishment from divine words. It's no wonder, then, that the last command Jesus gives his disciples was to go into all the world and speak God.

The words kept coming even after Jesus' execution. A band of distraught disciples sat huddled together in defeat. They discussed what to do next, as if anyone knew. Then it happened. A holy wind swept through the room, and they breathed it into their lungs, and they exhaled words they did not know they knew. Tongues of fire sparked and strange words emerged from their mouths. The chorus of noises swirled throughout the neighborhood with such intensity that a crowd rushed to investigate.

Words usher in every transformative moment in biblical history.

The commotion eventually died down, but the talking did not cease. These followers of Jesus traveled to every corner of the globe speaking God to all who would listen. In some places, people grew annoyed or even angry at their chatter, but this would not stop them. Whenever they were instructed to sit down and shut up, they replied phlegmatically, "We cannot keep from speaking about what we have seen and heard."[12]

God could have launched this new era of history in an infinite number of ways, but God chose a linguistic miracle. In fact, words usher in *every* transformative moment in biblical history, which may explain why the apostles Peter and James often talked about talking in their letters. And why seven times in his letter to the Romans, Paul asks, "What shall we *say*?"[13]

The earliest Christians were almost all Jewish, but have you considered why most today are not? It's partly because the first believers made a decision about which language they would use to communicate their good news. In perhaps a moment of divine illumination, they selected common Greek, the lingua franca of the Roman Empire and a language of immense cultural influence in the Mediterranean. Had they chosen Hebrew instead, Christianity may never have become the world's largest religion and might have been limited to a small Jewish sect.

Ancient followers of the Jesus Way revered sacred words and knew that speaking God should be an intentional act. They understood that the language of faith—like any language and perhaps *more* than any language—provides the glue that binds a community together.

A quote often attributed to Saint Francis of Assisi goes something like this: "Preach the gospel at all times; if necessary use words." Whoever said it, the phrase is meant to convey that Christianity is best seen as a lived practice and example, rather than a lecture. It means that Christianity is made credible by works of love, compassion, service.

This is all true. Yet, words are far more necessary than this quote leads us to believe. The Christian faith would not exist—it cannot exist—without words. They are the way the religion produces progeny.[14]

Someone spoke and an interest was piqued.

Someone spoke and a heart fluttered.

Someone spoke and a spirit stirred.

Someone spoke and a new convert was born.

If you are a part of the Christian tradition, have you ever wondered how that became so? It is because someone spoke to someone who spoke to someone who spoke to someone about God. This transmission of words rippled across time and space until someone in that chain spoke words to you. The Christian faith was designed to replicate itself, in part, through the act of speaking.

Sacred words are containers that carry information about deep and often invisible realities. They help us describe, albeit imperfectly, what we believe. Words allow us to whisper encouragement over the God-loved downtrodden, and we use them to pray and to preach and to praise. When we stop speaking God, the future of the Christian religion itself hangs in the balance.

But in the midst of our struggles to speak God—struggles that are not unique to our generation—somehow God always finds a way to break through and keep God's people talking. If God's people have revived their vocabulary in past eras, surely there is a way to stoke these fires yet again.

4

The Possibility of Revival

Three blocks from my Brooklyn apartment, a large brick structure reaches toward the sky. Built in 1869, the building housed Saint Vincent de Paul Catholic Church. During the twentieth century, the congregants of this parish were predominantly Irish Americans. Later, a group of Armenians took it over. By the early 2000s, rain leaked through holes left by missing shingles and a tree had sprouted in the bell tower. So the Brooklyn diocese packed up its sacred objects, including the three-thousand-pound bronze bell, and sold the building to developers.

Today, the former church has been transformed into luxury lofts with two bedroom apartments renting for $5,500 per month or more. *Cha-ching.* Residents snore where the faithful once prayed and shower where children were baptized. Stained-glass windows adorn the living spaces in the most desirable units, washing living rooms with the same colored light that once graced parishioners.

The building formerly known as Saint Vincent de Paul Catholic Church is a metaphor for the way many in cities like New York live: surrounded by religious symbols but not giving them more than a moment's consideration. Religious icons pepper our metropolis—from stately cathedrals to the meditating Buddha that sits in a reflecting pool at my nearest Thai restaurant—but a secular impulse still seems to animate the city.

Other than what I saw on a few vacations, most of my preconceptions about New York were derived from films. The city's midcentury glory shone through the songs of three sailors in *On the Town*. Oliver Stone's *Wall Street* made moving there seem like buying a winning lottery ticket. And the romantic tales of *Serendipity* and *You've Got Mail* tempted me to fall in love with falling in love under the city lights.

But it doesn't take much time living here to realize that the city of these films is a fiction. New York is far more complex than those flat images, and its religious side is no exception. People here are not antagonistic toward religion. Many would describe themselves as "spiritual," though most do not attend a church, mosque, temple, or synagogue. Working for corporations takes precedence over corporate worship, social lives are more valued than spiritual disciplines, and most people save their Sunday-best clothing for Monday through Friday.

This description is not unique to New York City. Many places in America increasingly look similar.

When we stop speaking God, we risk becoming like Saint Vincent de Paul Church in my neighborhood—a husk of a community with trees in the bell towers, struggling to recall the message we have to offer the world. We'll have lost our vocabulary and the ancient wisdom it contains. In this ceasing, we sever our link to the past and are subsumed by the dominant culture. Still, all is not lost. The further I dove into my study of linguistics, the more I realized that embers of hope remained.

If you ask linguists how many languages are spoken on planet Earth, the answer will range from four thousand to seven thousand,[1] but all agree the number is declining with haste. When speakers die, their children and grandchildren must determine whether to carry on their ancestor's tongue or let it die with them. Many young people opt for more broadly spoken languages over their native tongues, causing languages to evaporate at incredible rates. At least twenty-five languages vanish each year, and according to some estimates, the number of languages spoken around the globe will be reduced by half by the end of this century, if not sooner.[2]

When the speakers of a language fail to transfer it to the next generation before passing away, linguists declare it a "dead language."[3] Physical causes of death are among the most common. If a group of speakers is wiped out, then the people's native tongue vanishes with them. No one speaks Hittite anymore for a singular reason: the Hittite civilization was obliterated.

Genocide is also linguicide. In El Salvador in 1932, for example, more than twenty-five thousand natives were slaughtered in the massacre known as the *gran matanza*. Two languages, Cacaopera and Lenca, perished as well. In addition to massacres, physical causes may include natural disasters, deadly diseases, and migrations.[4]

Economic motivating factors are even more common in the modern era. Certain languages come to dominate various industries over time. This convinces some cultures to select a trade language, foisting it upon all who wish to engage in large-scale commerce. These trade languages become known as "killer languages" because they create sweeping pressure to abandon native tongues and focus on becoming fluent in the standardized parlance.[5]

When the Aboriginal people in Australia began integrating into modern cities, they became bilingual. They spoke Aboriginal languages only at home, in tribal ceremonies, and when they hunted and fished with their families. Over time, economic pressures pushed them further into more lucrative enterprises, spurring the decline of hunting, fishing, and ritual practices. Very few people speak Aborigine languages today, and these tongues will likely be extinct soon.[6]

We must recognize that Christians have often contributed to linguicide in many cultures through missionary efforts. From Spanish missionaries in Peru to Franciscan missionaries in Mexico to Jesuit missionaries in Paraguay, and even American missionaries to North America's indigenous people, Christians have often propagated the language of their origin over others for the purpose of evangelizing. Thankfully, recent years and developments in Bible translation have brought new thinking to believers who want to speak God to those who don't share their faith or tongue.

> **Preserving a decaying language is like preserving a decomposing corpse. It requires great skill and hard work, and few people care enough to do it.**

Whenever a language begins to decline, social pressure usually hastens its demise. Fading languages lose prestige and become uncool. Kids will tease classmates who use it on the playground. Teenagers feel pressure to replace it with the languages spoken by celebrities and sung by pop musicians. And adults feel an odd amount of shame so that they often refuse to utter the language in public.[7]

Preserving a decaying language is like preserving a decomposing corpse. It requires great skill and hard work, and few people care enough to do it. Part of the problem is that when a language falls out of use, it becomes impractical. You might be able to speak it with a few people from your family or tribe, but you won't be able to order a coffee or purchase an SUV with those words. The most basic tasks become tractor beams pulling you away from your native language.

Resisting feels futile.

The more I researched why native languages die, the more I noticed parallels with the decline of sacred speech. In the late twentieth century, many young believers reacted against their parents' faith, which felt culturally irrelevant, socially exclusive, and politically partisan. They didn't want to sound anything like their parents, but they didn't know how to be Christians and sound like anything else. So speaking God itself became uncommon and uncool. As American culture grew more secular and pluralistic, speaking God felt inappropriate for professional settings and better uttered only in private.

A related trend has accelerated the decline: waning church attendance, particularly among young people. As many as seven thousand American churches close their doors each year.[8] Most of the churches that remain in business aren't experiencing substantial growth. New religious communities are being planted, of course, but these are not bridging the gap. More than two million Americans give up on church attendance every year.[9]

Optimistic church advocates have long countered this dire data by noting that about 40 percent of Americans still "say" they attend church regularly. But demographers have dug deeper in recent years, using time diaries and other research tools. We now know that far fewer Americans—perhaps fewer than 20 percent—actually attend church despite what they tell pollsters.[10]

Not only are fewer Americans attending church, but the committed ones are showing up less frequently. When I was a child, we attended church on Tuesday and Wednesday evenings and twice on Sunday. When special events arose, our family might pull into that parking lot five or six times in a week. Dad kept spare shirts and ties in a church closet for times when he needed an end-of-day wardrobe change, and my mom tucked a makeup bag under a bathroom sink in case she was in a hurry. If I didn't have time to eat between church events, I'd sometimes sneak off to snack on a handful of communion wafers and some holy grape juice.

Today, the average church attender probably shows up once per week for a couple of hours and no more. Many more attend sporadically or not at all. And this matters because churches are places to speak God.

Linguists note that as a community grows more diffuse and gathers less frequently, the risk of losing its common language increases. People in a community speak their language more frequently and with greater sophistication when they spend time together. So when they do not gather as often, they do not speak as often. If this happens long enough, the fire flickers out and the language dies.

When we speak God, we are not just voicing letters strung together in a certain order. We are handling containers of spiritual knowledge. Countless generations have picked up these words and wrestled with their meanings. Their experiences force us to re-ask old questions and brainstorm new ones as we seek to understand the world we live in and the world we cannot see.

"Each [language] provides its own cognitive toolkit, and encapsulates the knowledge and worldview developed over thousands of years within a culture," one linguist writes. "Each contains a way of perceiving, categorizing and making meaning in the world, an invaluable guidebook developed and honed by our ancestors."[11]

When a language dies, knowledge dies with it.[12] This is troubling when we consider the decline of sacred speech, yet there is still reason for hope.

If living languages can die, then dying languages can be revived.

While sacred speech is fading, it's unlikely to die out like Sumerian or Ugaritic. Not in the near future, at least. Enough people still speak God both throughout America and, increasingly, in non-Western countries in places like the global South. But if current trends persist, the vocabulary of faith may become like Latin—still learned in some settings but seldom verbalized. Or perhaps its destiny will resemble Coptic, uttered only in religious ceremonies by a faithful few and almost no one else.

Such fates are only slightly better than total extinction. Imagine a world where *grace* mostly refers to prima ballerinas and *sin* conjures an image of molten chocolate cake. Envision a reality in which *God* is only shouted when your hammer misses the nail and *saved* just refers to what you do with your 401(k).

This depressing future is not a foregone conclusion. Throughout my research, I kept stumbling onto stories of what linguists call "comeback languages," which are tongues that declined and somehow returned from the brink of extinction. Once a community of speakers realizes that their language is in peril, they must decide if they want to save it. And some are successful.

Hebrew is the most famous example of a comeback language by far. The language received its death certificate in the second century AD, then used only for liturgy and prayer. In the last part of the nineteenth century, a group of Jewish speakers led by Eliezer Ben-Yehuda decided to begin speaking it again in order to revitalize it. Today, millions speak Hebrew, and it's the national language of the nation of Israel. As historian Cecil Roth once noted, "Before Ben-Yehuda, Jews *could* speak Hebrew; after him, they *did*."[13]

Similar to Hebrew, the Yiddish tongue is on the rise after a period of steep decline (although my Jewish friends tell me that *kvetching* has never been on the decline, and I'll always be a *schmuck* no matter how language evolves.) Used by European Jews through the early twentieth century, Yiddish nearly vanished due in part to the Holocaust. But the tongue saw a revival in the last part of the last century, thanks to the efforts of prominent Yiddish speakers and writers.[14]

In 1978, a Polish-born Jewish writer named Isaac Bashevis Singer won the Nobel Prize in Literature even though he wrote only in Yiddish. When a journalist once asked Singer why he penned books in a dying language, the author replied, "I like ghost stories, and I also believe in resurrection."[15]

The Jewish people aren't the only people group resuscitating dying languages. The Irish language was nearly extinct at the end of the nineteenth century, for example, but now boasts nearly two million speakers. Hawaiian almost fell silent in the 1800s, but it is now surging, with the number of native speakers increasing by twelvefold from 1997 to 2007.[16] Efforts to revitalize Welsh and Galician are also making strides.

These stories caused hope to take root again. After, all Isaac Singer isn't the only one who believes in resurrection.

If living languages can die, then dying languages can be revived.

5

How (Not) to Speak God

My shoes were soaking from the spring rainstorm I'd just endured, and I struggled to catch my breath. I'd raced to the subway stop, barely missing the last train due to a slothy passenger who had blocked the turnstile while trying to locate her MetroCard. My meeting was scheduled to start in a half hour, and it would take me at least that long to get there.

As I stepped onto the platform, a train pulled into the station—and I froze. As a newbie New Yorker, I'd failed to follow the cardinal rule of riding the subway: always decide where you're going and how you'll get there *before* you leave, rather than after. *Should I get on the J train? Or was I supposed to ride the M?* Fumbling for my phone, I Googled an MTA transit map and realized that, yes, I indeed needed to take the J. But the train doors had closed by the time I figured it out. My lack of planning and slow response cost me ten minutes I couldn't afford to lose.

My heart was thumping by the time the next J train arrived. Taking a seat, I exhaled with relief and retrieved a book. I would be a smidge late, but I couldn't do anything about it at this point. I was a slave to the punctuality of MTA now and might as well enjoy a moment of solitude and silence.

It's odd to speak of quiet and aloneness when you're riding a train packed with perfect strangers. But the label is not inaccurate.

One of the only places in New York where you're unlikely to hear words spoken is in a subway train. Residents know that these trains are for traveling, not places for making new friends. An eerie silence settles as fellow passengers avoid eye contact and speech unless absolutely necessary. Though a crowd of people may surround you, you behave as if you are the last person living. (Subway sociologists call this odd behavior "civil inattention." And, yes, a subway sociologist is actually a thing.)

In the hush, I focused on the pages of my book as we passed one stop and then two and then five. Knowing that the sixth stop was mine, I closed my books, gathered my belongings, and disembarked . . . only to realize that I had boarded the eastbound train instead of the westbound. Eyes fixed on my watch, my frustration grew. Few things fluster me quite like tardiness, especially when I feel that lateness reflects poorly on my vocational competence.[1]

I finally caught a lucky break. A westbound J train traveling in the opposite direction was on the adjacent track. I raced across the platform and barely slipped between the closing doors. But too much time had passed going the opposite direction. I missed my meeting.

I wish I could say that this was the only time I'd made such a mistake, but that would be untrue. I boarded wrong trains and traveled in wrong directions and missed connections at least a dozen times during my first year living in New York. Each misadventure was more embarrassing than the one before.

The kaleidoscope of colors, numbers, and letters on a subway map appears daunting to newcomers like me. But upon boarding a train, a long-time resident can tell you exactly where you'll end up.

It's like jumping onto Interstate 70 in Kansas. The landscape looks the same whether traveling east or west. Without a GPS or ability to read the road signs, outsiders have no idea whether they're heading to the mountains of Utah or the Maryland coast. But a local resident riding shotgun can predict your destination just by paying attention to which farms and fields they're passing.

Whenever we take a journey—on a subway or a highway or a walking trail—we are faced with three possible options: We can stay where we are. We can travel in the wrong direction. Or we can forge a path forward toward our desired endpoint. The decision we make will determine the destination at which we arrive.

What is true of physical travel is also true of the journey to speak God from scratch. Whenever a language begins to die, its speakers can choose among at least three response paths.

———

First, speakers can circle the wagons and protect their sacred vocabulary. This is the most natural reaction because it requires less energy and imagination. But it amounts to doing nothing, to freezing, to staying where one stands, immovable and still. I call this approach *fossilization* because it treats words as if they were locked in space and time rather than alive.

My friend Jerry works at a café in a place New Yorkers do their best to avoid: Times Square. He can be found serving mimosas and eggs Benedict on Sunday mornings because the weekend tips are good and he doesn't have anywhere else to be. A decade ago, Jerry could be found in church on those days, but he quit institutional religion after church leaders told him he was no longer welcome.

His crime? Questioning their accepted definitions of certain words.

Jerry first encountered church in young adulthood, and the experience was both wonderful and weird. He dove into conversations about supernatural forces and the meaning of life and the nature of humanity. He began reading the Bible and even tried praying in the mornings before his shift started.

When Jerry attended a new members' orientation class a few months in, he started squirming when church leaders spoke about "salvation." For more than an hour, they explained all the linear steps in how the process of salvation worked. The more they explained their thinking, the less convinced Jerry felt. He raised his hand and offered another way to think about it, but his ideas were dismissed.

He met with a minister a week later to dialogue about the matter, but he was told he was wrong and should read his Bible and pray about it. So Jerry did. But in seeking confirmation, his varying perspective became cemented. When he talked with other members about the matter, he was labeled a troublemaker. Before long, he received a phone call from a pastor who told him that if he refused to stop "stirring up trouble" he would need to leave the church. Better to lose one of the congregants than entertain the possibility that his definition of a sacred word might be open for debate. Welcoming questions allows for challenges to long-established theological systems—and in many churches, such explorations can't be entertained.

In the past couple of years, I've shared the idea that spiritual words are dying with many pastors. The solution they propose is almost always the same: return to the ancient roots of our spiritual vocabulary. The problem is that the origin of most words isn't fixed or even known, and therefore, a single original meaning is difficult to pinpoint. Often when someone talks about the "original meaning" of a word, she is just referring to whichever modern interpretation she has accepted.[2]

They believe this approach will save spiritual words. Fossilized, though, these terms drive God-speakers like Jerry away.

When a community realizes their native tongue is endangered, their natural instincts often lead them to the worst possible response. Perhaps it is driven by sentimentalism. Or fear. Or what I call the Hezekiah syndrome.

King Hezekiah was a well-intentioned, righteous man and the ruler of Judah. During his reign, he enacted reforms to preserve the temple worship in Jerusalem and helped people discover the beauty and wonder of God's laws.

> **Building a fence around our spiritual vocabulary accomplishes little if there's trouble inside the camp.**

Though Hezekiah's name means "God is my strength" in Hebrew, the book of 2 Kings exposes his weakness. Flattered by a visit from the envoy of a Babylonian prince, Hezekiah gave the entourage a VIP tour complete with backstage passes. He showed them the palace and the armory and the storehouses that kept all of Israel's treasures. Hezekiah basked in his accomplishments, but he educated the enemy like a fool.

After the king bid them adieu, the prophet Isaiah popped in for a visit.

"Who were those men and what did they see?" the prophet asked.

"That was the prince of the most powerful nation on earth," Hezekiah replied. "He wanted to admire all we've amassed, so I showed him everything. I gave him a grand tour of all our treasures."[3]

Exasperated, Isaiah delivered the hard news: The time will come, he said, when every jewel, coin, and gold bar in Hezekiah's palace will be lugged off to Babylon. The country that so easily stroked Hezekiah's ego would destroy his empire. Even some of his own descendants would be taken away and become slaves in the palace of the Babylonian king.[4]

The prophecy should have devastated Hezekiah who had just been told that the dynasty he spent his lifetime constructing would be swept away by a foreign invader. The most important treasure a king has—his legacy—gone. Yet, Hezekiah responded with shocking words: "'The word of the LORD you have spoken is good,' Hezekiah replied. For he thought, 'Will there not be peace and security *in my lifetime?*'"[5]

We're all prone to this type of thinking. When trouble is coming but is still far off, our natural instincts can lead to inaction—especially when it seems the worst effects may not hit until after we're gone. Complacency overtakes courage. The status quo reigns.

In the case of sacred words, this approach seeks to save the ailing language by attempting to protect certain words and preserve "traditional" meanings. But it ends up destroying them by pushing doubters, dissenters, and curious speakers to the margins or straight out the exit.

Speakers often choose fossilization because it is easier than evaluating the problems that have led to the crisis, which may implicate the community and its leaders. Or maybe because an active response would mean admitting that the meanings they've attached to words no longer work, which could destabilize their tidy theological system. For those of us who love sacred words, letting go of what we've known is difficult, even if these ways are broken.

Unfortunately, fossilization does nothing to address how poorly some of our old words and definitions are working. Building a fence around our spiritual vocabulary accomplishes little if there's trouble inside the camp.

———

Second, when a language is in decline, speakers can stop using any words they feel have become tainted and replace these terms with less offensive expressions.

A few years ago, in the Town Hall Theater just near Times Square, author and former pastor Rob Bell gathered a few hundred eager listeners to deliver a lecture as part of his thirty-one-city "Everything Is Spiritual" tour. During the course of the evening, he quoted the Sufi mystic Rumi and the Catholic thinker Pierre Teilhard de Chardin. He spoke about love, grace, energy, and "the soul of the universe." But I was surprised at how little he said "God."

When I interviewed Bell following the show, he told me that, after talking about God for decades, he finds himself saying the G-word far less these days. He said his shift in focus is driven mostly by a desire for clarity—communicating what he means rather than playing into people's preconceptions. After all, he suggested, *God* has become such a muddled and volatile word.

"When a word becomes too toxic and too abused and too associated with ideas and understandings that aren't true to the mystery behind the mystery," Bell said, "it's important to set it aside and search for new and better ways to talk about it."[6]

God has been given new names before, Bell explained. "Jesus talked about his Father. Moses spoke of Yahweh. [The Christian theologian] Paul Tillich wrote about the ground of our being. The apostle Paul referred to the Theos," he told me. "Others throughout the ages and across traditions have spoken of wind and fire and clothing and whispers— it's all language, metaphor, our feeble attempts to put words to the ineffable."

Bell illustrates the second way speakers can respond to an ailing language: *substitution*. This approach identifies problematic or triggering words and purges them from the sacred lexicon. The words are sometimes replaced with less offensive terms and phrases uninhibited by cultural baggage. This is often the chosen path of those with innovative spirits and progressive theologies.

While it may be necessary to avoid certain words in exceptional situations, *substitution* is ultimately unsustainable. It often shrinks the vocabulary of faith, rather than expands it. *Substitution* avoids linguistic problems, rather than resolving them, and struggles to root itself in a sacred scripture where these words remain despite our discomfort.[7]

Just after I heard Bell speak, I attended a writing conference at Princeton Theological Seminary and heard popular author Barbara Brown Taylor give a disclaimer that she might not say "God" often enough for some attendees. Later, she told me she began speaking God's name less after she conducted an experiment: She asked a dozen students at Piedmont College, the liberal arts school where she taught religion, to write down on an index card what they meant when they said "God." The answers were as varied as the faces in her classroom.

"I realized the word *God* was no more revealing of what the speaker meant by it than words such as *big, dark,* or *good,*" she said.

These days, Taylor told me, she was having as much trouble pinning down the word's meaning as her students. She is spending more time with people for whom the word has a negative association. For some, "God . . . is the name of someone they once thought they loved who is no longer there . . . a symbol of ultimatums, judgment, rebuff."

Our inability to dialogue about the Divine can make us feel inadequate, but we often ignore these feelings. After all, as Taylor says, *God* is just an expression to help us discuss something difficult to describe with words.

"It may be a finger pointing to the moon, but it is not the moon," Taylor says. "It seems more helpful to use some other fingers to point to the moon, using the language of creation, suffering, longing, belonging, joy—and letting my readers supply 'God' when that is the right word for them."[8]

If I gather a half dozen friends around a table and say "God," images will flash into all their minds—each one unique, many incompatible with others. Some think of God as a disciplining dad who is rigid and rules based. Others envision God as a kind of heavenly bellhop whose job is to make people happy, healthy, and wealthy. A few take an artistic approach, envisioning Creator or Maker. Others imagine God as an impersonal force.[9]

In a moment when so many sacred words have become tainted or toxic or confusing or empty, one response would be to identify the most problematic words and stop using them, substituting fresh phrases for tired and tainted terms.

As Kevin Kelly, a futurist and cofounder of *Wired* magazine, observed, "Part of the challenge of religion today is that it is really locked into a vocabulary of a thousand years ago. We need new language for talking about these very ancient truths."[10]

Kelly isn't the first person to identify such a problem or propose such a solution. Novelist Thornton Wilder noticed the early stages of this problem in the midst of the Great Depression. Religion was failing to articulate a meaningful message to a society immersed in poverty and despair. Cornerstone terms that were meant to be uplifting, he noted, had become loaded with negative associations and fashioned into weapons of judgment. They had become "signposts for ways of life that are repressive, confining, and guilt-inducing."

"The revival in religion will be a rhetorical problem—new persuasive words for defaced or degraded ones," Wilder said.[11]

When the words of faith fall into disrepair, many respond by refusing to speak them and hunting for more capable language. Many of our most cherished terms appear to some as four-letter words. A word may become so toxic, so tarnished, so misused, that it seems impossible to redeem. Nothing is left but a crunchy husk, a memory of something that once had value.

Substitution seeks to save a dying language by pitching problematic or empty words and searching for new language to replace them. It's a well-intentioned but unsustainable approach to bring about a revival of the language we use in prayer, worship, blogs, articles, and books. Too many spiritual words are tainted in some way. If we throw out every last one, we won't have much on which to build again. Substitution cannot be scaled.

Those who employ substitution may counter that the concept remains even if the word has been replaced. But most religions have spoken languages with a sacred text. There's a reason Christians, as well as Jews and Muslims, have been referred to as People of the Book. We can stop using a word in prayer, sermons, and spiritual conversations, but we end up bumping into it the moment we return to our scriptures or the sayings of our religious ancestors.

Eliminating a certain arrangement of letters does little to rectify the tension we feel with the *idea* those words are pointing to.

God-speakers who squirm when they hear a word don't object inherently to stringing together specific letters in a specific order. We have a problem with the meaning behind the word.[12] Eliminating a certain arrangement of letters does little to rectify the tension we feel with the *idea* those words are pointing to.

As one linguist has noted, "If you remove 'retarded' from the dictionary, people tell us, then no one will ever smear someone as 'retarded' ever again, because that word is no longer a word. . . . [But] removing a word from the dictionary doesn't do away with the thing the word refers to specifically, or even tangentially."[13]

We may choose not to use the word *retarded* because it is unnecessarily hurtful to those with mental challenges. But we should not pretend that purging this word from our vocabulary solves our collective insensitivity to those people or their problems. The hard work still remains. We have only fooled ourselves into thinking we have solved a problem that still very much exists.

Many sacred words are foundational phrases in the language of faith that can't be extracted without altering the faith itself, and they are not irreparably tainted. Surely, *God* counts. As my friend, the Jesuit priest James Martin, says, "God is at the heart of religion."[14] This seems like a foundational word for followers of any of the world's great faiths. Religion without God is like a human without a heart.

Bell, Taylor, Kelly, and Thornton are correct that modern believers face a rhetorical problem. They are also correct that those invested in the future of faith have no choice but to rethink the way we speak God. But substitution is a handful of Band-Aids for a chronically ill vocabulary. And fossilization repels doubters, skeptics, and cynics by protecting words that may need reimagining. Luckily, we don't have to bury our heads in the sand or dispose of all the words we struggle to speak.

A better way exists.

———————

The third possible response requires speakers to muster the courage to play with sacred words, despite their complexities and histories and trappings. This approach recognizes that sacred words have often been shaped by our gender and geography, interests and prejudices, race and class.[15] So it allows those holy terms to grow and expand and take on new meanings. I call this approach *transformation* because it recognizes the fluctuating nature of language.

3 RESPONSES TO A LANGUAGE IN PERIL

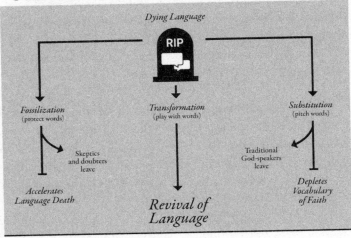

One principle on which all linguists seem to agree is that, over time, every language will either change or die.[16]

Transformation is inherent in language.

In his book *Studies in Words,* C. S. Lewis likens the meaning of a word to the growth of a tree: "As everyone knows, words constantly take on new meanings." New meanings do not usually obliterate old ones but are instead connected to them. Lewis said this process works like a tree growing new branches, which then sprout other branches, and so on.[17]

While a new branch may overshadow an old one, it doesn't always. Every twig is connected to a branch and each branch to the trunk. Even if we can't trace a word back to the original trunk because the history of a word has some gaps in it, Lewis's point is that "The tree that exists in speakers' minds at a particular time need not match the tree that shows the growth of the word's meaning throughout history."[18] Lewis's thoughts are uncontroversial among linguists[19] and invite us to embrace a new way of engaging sacred language—one that gives us permission to play with words, allowing their meanings to transform as we use them.[20]

Transformation is a riskier road and a more difficult path to be sure. But if fossilization turns off younger generations of God-speakers, and if substitution neglects the inspired text and backbone of the Christian faith, transformation might mark the way forward.

6

The Way Forward

A consistent rumble echoed from underneath my seat in row seventeen, while naked oak trees flickered past my window. The smooth whisper-motion of the train car left me hypnotized and buried in thought about the task that lay before me. Still somewhat skeptical about the transformational approach to language, I decided to call in reinforcements. So I hopped on a high-speed Amtrak train from New York's Penn Station to New Haven, Connecticut.

Professor Joel Baden, a renowned professor at Yale Divinity School and a specialist in the Hebrew language, has a sculpted beard and a laugh that spills out like a fountain. His affable approach to life and keen insights instantly drew me in. In New Haven, we spent the afternoon discussing how ancient Jewish people spoke God.

Baden explained that ancient Jews did not treat sacred words like most modern Christians, as static objects with fixed definitions. Ancient Jews believed words were malleable. These terms didn't convey a solitary meaning, but rather many meanings at the same time. Rather than immovable rocks, they were more like clay. Solid but shapeable.

The ancient Jewish approach to language was, in part, born out of necessity. From a linguistic standpoint, Hebrew has a much more limited lexicon than English. So every Hebrew word has more nuance and many more potential meanings than an English word. For example, Baden recounted a story in which one of his students translated the Hebrew word for "anger" as "resentment." This was acceptable because Hebrew doesn't have a word for "resentment."

Theological motivations are tucked into this ancient Jewish approach to language. They believed that language was a gift from God through which God was revealed through the Scriptures. If God is infinite and mysterious and complex, then it stands to reason that revelation from God would be similarly enigmatic. Just as we learn more about the Divine with every encounter, so too we can peel back the layers of sacred speech as we interact with it. If God put a word there, the Jews believed, we should try to get every last drop of meaning out of it.

> **Ancient Jews did not treat sacred words like most modern Christians, as static objects with fixed definitions. Ancient Jews believed words were malleable.**

"For ancient Jewish interpreters, the biblical text—every word, verse, and story—was meant to be *played* with. They attempted to mine every imaginable meaning," he said. "By applying different meanings, they would mine different principles. Any notion that the language of the Bible would have one meaning, in Judaism, doesn't make sense."[1]

Consider the word *love*. When the writer of Deuteronomy commands the people of God to "love the LORD your God with all your heart,"[2] the original meaning is different from the meaning later ascribed.

The word for "love" (אהבה) in Deuteronomy was used broadly in the ancient Near East in political treaties to describe enforced loyalty to the dominant party. According to Baden, a king would tell a vassal, "You are obligated to *love* me, which is to say, to be obedient to me." In this light, the verse comes across more like a threat than a thoughtful solicitation.

Ancient Jewish rabbis had no knowledge of these ancient treaties, Baden said, so they interpreted it allegorically, in the way that many early Christians did. Scholars eventually discovered this millennia later, Baden said, but the meaning of the word had already shifted.

Today's Christians think of this command in terms of emotional affection, rather than dutiful loyalty. This shift—perhaps informed by the romanticized romcom culture in which we live—is not inappropriate from a Hebrew standpoint, Baden said. Ancient Jews understood that words have many meanings, including some that have been lost and others that have not yet been found.[3]

The Hebrew word for "love" is one example among many that Baden offered. The word for "righteousness" or "to be in the right" was used originally to refer to a person in a courtroom who wins a case. The word for "convert" in the Hebrew Bible is the same as the word for "resident alien" or "stranger in the land." As with "love," these words morph with time.

> **When language brushes up against your life, you can peel back new layers and textures and shades.**

Baden confirmed that sacred language, like all languages, evolves over time.

In order to revive the vocabulary of faith, God-speakers need to have open mouths and open minds. They must be willing to use the language and also willing to allow the language to change. This is true of every comeback language—modern Hebrew, Yiddish, Irish, and Hawaiian all vary from their previous versions.[4] The grammar evolved, syntax shifted, meanings transformed, and new words sprouted.

The God who created with language and revealed with language and loves language chose to use language throughout history, knowing well the way it works. When language brushes up against your life, you can peel back new layers and textures and shades.

A transformational approach to speaking God gives me clam-hands. I prefer safety over scary, normal over new, regular over risky. All would be much easier if every sacred word had a uniform, universal, unchanging meaning. But this is just not how words work. The only way to revive the lexicon of faith is to revisit our most sacred terms, asking which ones need pruning, which ones need new life, which ones need space for a fresh shoot to emerge. For this, we must rely on two virtues that are in short supply these days: courage and imagination.

Playing with words like the ancient Jews and early Christians did may be a challenge for some, especially those of us who grew up with access to dictionaries. Millennia ago, no single authority stated, "This particular definition is what this word means, forever." Throughout most of history meanings were worked out in community with the help of discernment.

When the first dictionaries were published in the late 1500s and early 1600s, however, everything in the Western world began to shift. People now had an authoritative resource for the definitions of words. In the 1700s and 1800s, the field of grammar gained popularity. People began to develop systems of rules to govern language. These grammarians decided they wanted to "freeze [language] and keep it from changing further."[5] Among other reasons, writers knew that their works would have a shorter shelf life if words continued to morph as they naturally do.

As usage of dictionaries spread, the value placed on their contents rose.[6] A dictionary became "a hallowed leather-clad tome of truth and wisdom as infallible as God"[7] and "a book viewed with a level of respect normally accorded only to the Bible."[8]

The cultural consequences of dictionaries remain until today. Whenever we hear a word with a meaning we don't understand, we rush straight to a dictionary (if not in print then online).[9]

Kory Stamper, a lexicographer for Merriam-Webster, says language doesn't work like most assume. Since the rise of dictionaries, people (like her) sitting in dimly lit offices in Middle America have largely defined words for the rest of the world. And this is not an easy task. Though dictionaries give us the impression that a word's meaning is easy to discern, she says, "what appears to be a straightforward word ends up being a linguistic fun house" filled with prejudices, convictions, history, and baggage.[10]

Even still, dictionaries have given us the impression that words' meanings are fixed. When people go to the dictionary and look up the definition of a word like *love,* Stamper says, they expect to find an explanation of what love *is.*[11] But, as Stamper explains, dictionaries don't explain what words *mean.* They only tell us how words are *used.* Every word—*love* included—has many, often overlapping uses that will change over time.[12]

Modern Christians are children of both Merriam-Webster and King James. We often approach language like chemistry or algebra rather than like poetry or painting.

This misconception hasn't stopped the dictionary from reshaping the way we think about words—including sacred terms.[13]

As English moved away from notions of multiple meanings that ancient Jews and others accepted, they stopped playing with sacred words and ceased reimagining spiritual terms. The result: biblical language became locked in place. For example, many popular Bible translations, like the King James Version, became flat texts in which a single Greek or Hebrew word is always translated with corresponding English word, even though that word may mean different things based on context, geography, time, and culture.

Modern Christians are children of both Merriam-Webster and King James. We often approach language like chemistry or algebra rather than like poetry or painting. This suffocates sacred language, making it unrecognizable to the ancients of the Judeo-Christian tradition. We need a dose of courage and imagination to revive the vocabulary of faith.

———————

The writers of the Hebrew Bible stoked the fires of sacred linguistics with frequent wordplay. One of the earmarks of their imaginative approach is the frequent use of metaphor throughout the text. When writers employ metaphor, they use the language of approximation, or similarity, rather than precision. You can't look up a metaphor in a dictionary, define it, and then move on. You have to pick it up, wrestle with it, debate it. The metaphor means something—but its meaning can change.

Consider Hebrew writers' descriptions of the Divine. Malachi speaks of God as soap and as a silversmith. Jeremiah talks about God as a potter, teacher, and doctor. The psalmist talks about God as a mad dog, while Hosea speaks of God as a lion, leopard, and bear.[14] We don't know much about God's nose or sinus cavities, but the Hebrew Bible still speaks of God as "the one who smells."[15]

The New Testament authors follow suit, making liberal use of divine metaphors. Matthew speaks of God as both a fisherman and an employer, while the author of Romans speaks of God as a farmer. In John's gospel, God is wind; in John's Revelation, God is thunder.

The figurative language of the Bible beckons us into a larger conversation. It forces us to stop and pause—to engage our imaginations, not just our brains. While we accept these analogies, they illustrate an approach to language that's often different from our own.[16]

Ancient Jewish sages often instructed their students to imagine themselves at the foot of Mount Sinai receiving the Torah. For them, this was not a one-time event but an ongoing experience.[17] Every term in every passage was treated as if it ended in a question mark, rather than a period. These Jewish thinkers treated language not as a corpse but as a living being with which we are invited to dance.

Since Jesus was a Jew, we should not be surprised that he also took an imaginative approach to language. His primary mode of teaching was telling parables, which are "products of the imagination."[18] They are not direct communication, but indirect.[19] They still lead readers to truth, but they enter through a side door. Parables invite us to jump into the deep end and splash around in layers of meanings.

When Jesus and the New Testament writers refer to the Hebrew Bible, they often suggest a new way of understanding old words, unfolding fresh layers of meaning. Which is why many scholars believe that the New Testament itself is an imaginative genre of spiritual literature called midrash.[20] It's a collection of voices reinterpreting the Hebrew Bible and reimagining spiritual words, often in untraditional ways.[21]

Many Christians throughout the centuries continued this imaginative approach to the sacred text. Just pick up writing by a desert father or early mystics, who offered "slightly mocking and subversive commentary upon the officially approved forms of words for speaking about God."[22]

God-speakers throughout the centuries have often used their imaginations to employ a transformational approach to language, but modern Christians struggle to keep up this tradition. We have exchanged an imaginative, transformative approach for one rooted in "Greek philosophy, which seeks to define, distinguish, pare down."[23]

Given the age in which we live, it's no wonder we struggle to speak God imaginatively. But engaging our imaginations is the only way we can learn the discipline of playing with words and speak God from scratch. For when we engage our imaginations, we open wide waves of meaning and begin to revive that which is struggling to survive.

What does it mean to speak God from scratch? I guess that depends on whom you ask.

American Old Testament theologian Walter Brueggemann might tell you that it is like getting lost—then finding your way again. He notes that humans live in three basic movements.

Orientation is the place where everything makes sense. For many, this era of life occurs at the beginning of a spiritual journey, when sacred words and their corresponding meanings work well. Then something happens—an unspeakable tragedy, the stresses of adulthood, new evidence that shatters our presuppositions. We enter the pit of *disorientation,* where our spiritual vocabulary no longer seems adequate and we are tempted to abandon it altogether. But with courage, we enter *reorientation,* in which we find fresh ways to think of and speak of sacred realities.[24]

If you ask British New Testament scholar N. T. Wright what it means to speak God from scratch, he might tell you it is a little like returning home from a long journey, only to leave again. He compares sacred words to luggage we carry, which possess either positive or negative emotional triggers, depending on how they have been used. Many of these terms, he says, have become compressed packages into which we jam complicated and sometimes messy ideas.

These linguistic suitcases were often packed long ago and left untouched. They served us well on our journeys, but when the seasons change, our needs morph. What has been *packed* must be *unpacked* and then *repacked*—perhaps in a different order.

"Too much debate about scriptural authority [has taken] the form of people hitting one another with locked suitcases. It is time to unpack our shorthand doctrines, to lay them out and inspect them," Wright says.

"Long years in a suitcase may have made some of the contents go moldy. They will benefit from fresh air, and perhaps a hot iron."[25]

If you ask Franciscan mystic Richard Rohr what it means to speak God from scratch, you might receive a similar answer. He says transformation and change occur in three stages. It begins with a period of *order,* when all our concepts about God and life and faith are placed into neat, tidy containers.

When life's vagaries blindside us, we are thrown into a period of *disorder.* During this stage, we begin questioning assumptions behind the words we've used and whether the meanings we've accepted need to be reimagined. This period grows us up, but it cannot last forever.

Human consciousness only evolves, Rohr says, when we move into the *reorder* stage. We reassemble what we've known to be true with *what we've learned to be true.* The same words exist within our lexicon, but now they contain more texture and color and nuance. If we are brave enough to move through all stages, we realize that our most sacred words have matured alongside us.[26]

Though these three Christian thinkers are separated by geography, theology, and culture, their approaches to spiritual formation are almost identical.

> Orientation > Disorientation > Reorientation
> Packing > Unpacking > Repacking
> Order > Disorder > Reorder

In order to speak God from scratch, we begin with what we have accepted. Then, we break it down, challenging our preconceptions. Finally, we build it back up in a way that is more helpful, richer, and beautiful.

Conservative God-speakers often remain in the first stage. They don't want to get lost because they believe they are already home. They don't want to unpack their luggage because they like the order, the tidiness. They may become overprotective of sacred terms and allow them to fossilize.

Progressive God-speakers often get stuck in the second stage.[27] They have deconstructed everything until they become lost among the pieces. Their postmodern minds question everything and trust nothing. They see spirituality—and its vocabulary—as infinitely gray and unclear. They pitch sacred words, substituting them with other terms they hope will serve them better. But often, the disorder becomes a black hole of uncertainty.

The bravest and best God-speakers move through all three stages. They identify the meaning of the sacred word as they've known it. Then they confront problems with this meaning—the ways it harms themselves and others as well as the ways their ethnicity, geography, chronology, and blind spots have influenced it. Finally, they muster the courage to reimagine a better and truer way of understanding the holy term.

———————

Speaking God from scratch means planting the vocabulary of faith in the fertile soil of the present moment so it can come back to life and even grow into something more beautiful than we first imagined.

After moving to New York, I realized the need to play with the words I'd unconsciously been avoiding. I decided to begin living aware of the linguistic tensions I felt. I refused to place sacred terms in liquid amber, fossilizing them and accepting the status quo. I committed to keep playing with the lexicon of faith. When I stumbled across a word that I previously resisted or that I had become overly familiar with, I would stop to notice it. I would pause and ponder it. Each time I encountered a term that made me squirm or prompted confusion, I named the meaning I'd given it, confronted that meaning's shortcomings, and then reimagined how I might understand the word afresh.

The chapters that follow represent my attempt to play with some of my most- and least-favorite sacred words. My word choices are incomplete and subjective, and I feel that they chose me rather than the other way around.

If my reflections don't sit well with you at first glance, don't worry. I am not trying to create a definitive spiritual dictionary, and I don't expect you to agree with every line you read. I encourage you to do what I have done. Dream about what sacred words might mean for *you* in the here and now.

Maybe you count yourself among the majority who has quietly, perhaps unknowingly, swept the vocabulary of faith under the rug. You also struggle to articulate what you believe and love, to describe the divine stirrings you feel. When you stare up at the stars, you wonder if the vocabulary you've inherited is more like the infinite blackness or the meteors that quietly speed across the sky. Maybe you, too, need spiritual speech therapy.

No matter where you find yourself, the most important thing about learning (or relearning) a vocabulary of faith is to remember that, in the words of Reynolds Price, "language is vehicle, almost never destination."[28] When we speak, we aren't just saying something—we're pointing to something. In the case of sacred language, we're pointing to meaning, to identity, to transcendence, and ultimately, to God.

Are you ready to speak God from scratch?

Then turn the page.

May the spark of holy words kindle a flame in your mind and on your tongue, and may you find your voice again.

FINDING OUR VOICES AGAIN

To open any part of one's faith, especially its prayers and holy words, to intense scrutiny is to know, even before the fact, that some things are going to change as a result. Some beloved concept will be slaughtered. Some startling and aberrant truth will push to the surface, making a rift in an otherwise smooth fabric of belief. Some treasured consolation will be snatched away as less than mature.

—Phyllis Tickle

7

Yes: Sacred Affirmations and Necessary Nos

At thirteen, Zach held the dubious honor of being my closest friend. We attended church and school together. We built tree houses, imagined our sticks were rifles, and snuck into the woods to smoke cigarettes that older kids had smuggled to us. Our weekends were spent at his house playing *The Legend of Zelda* and guzzling untold liters of Mountain Dew. When his parents fell asleep, we tiptoed down to the basement, where we watched the scrambled color bars of the Playboy Channel hoping for a moment of clarity during which we could glimpse naked bodies.

As an awkward, overweight teenager, I didn't have many friends to spare. Actually, Zach was just about the only one. So when he told me we couldn't hang out anymore, I rattled like a tuning fork.

I learned later that his new girlfriend didn't think I was cool enough to hang out with them—a point difficult to dispute—so she delivered an ultimatum: her or me. I didn't stand a chance.

I begged him to please, please reconsider, but he didn't even pause to deliberate: "No."

The word rang in my ears like the trumpets of Judgment Day, and tears filled my eyes. I returned home. Loneliness followed. Depression descended. All because of a single word.

It's not much to look at, *no*. Just two measly letters that form a single syllable. Yet when a particular person says *no* at the wrong moment, that skinny word morphs into a looming marauder that will mug you where you stand.

The same year Zach derailed our friendship with a *no*, I spoke a life-altering *yes*. I said *yes* to faith and *yes* to God and *yes* to a life of wrestling with both. The moment I spoke that three-letter word, I felt like a newborn infant with my whole life ahead of me. (Maybe that's why some people refer to spiritual conversion moments as being "born again.") Something about uttering this word changed the way I spoke and the way I heard others.

I paid attention to terms I'd taken for granted before. I eavesdropped on adults talking about spiritual matters and hung on every phrase. I read scripture verses with new curiosity. And listening to a sermon—previously a good excuse to play Hangman with my brothers—now left me scribbling copious notes.

During prayer, I paused for just the right phrases to express what I felt. Confession became less of a chore and more of a catharsis. I stumbled over sentences at first, but soon I spoke God as fluently as the grown-ups around me.

I attended a hymn-singing church, so many of the most important words in my life came paired with a melody. We were Baptist, so our song list differed from that of the Methodists next door, the Lutherans up the street, and the Episcopalians two towns over. But one song appeared in all of our hymnals, and it felt like a life anthem to me and many others:

> Amazing grace! How sweet the sound
> That saved a wretch like me!

I once was lost, but now I'm found;
Was blind, but now I see.

I self-identified as a wretch—both then and now—but something about the refrain always seems to rearrange the air around me.

In subsequent years, I've sung "Amazing Grace" in many places—at the Church of the Holy Sepulchre in Jerusalem, during the funeral of a friend killed by a drunk driver, in a thunderstorm at a Hampton Inn in Louisville, Kentucky. Each time I've sung or heard those words, I've felt like I was saying *yes* to God all over again.

Does "Amazing Grace," the most recognizable spiritual song in the English language, give religious communities a sense of purpose and meaning and mission? It certainly has for me, and all because I somehow mustered a droplet of courage and spoke a simple *yes*.

This tiny word doesn't seem substantial, much less holy. But reflecting on my early life has taught me that *yes* contains transformative power—even more than the omnipotent *no*.

No is an ending while yes marks a beginning.
No closes the door while yes kicks it open.
No warns me to turn back while yes beckons me forward.
No is an act of finality while yes is an expression of faith.

Even worse, a life of *no* makes us more judgmental. *No* can become the marker for determining if a person is good or bad, in or out. If left unchecked, our lives are shaped by "judging, controlling, and analyzing" instead of "seeing, tasting, and loving."[1]

Author Kathleen Norris notes that *no* is one of the first words infants learn to mutter, but *yes* is among the most righteous: "An unqualified 'yes' is a harder sell, to both children and adults. To say 'yes' is to make a leap of faith, to risk oneself in a new and often scary relationship. Not being quite sure of what we are doing, or where it will lead us, we try on assent, we commit ourselves to affirmation. With luck, we find that our efforts are rewarded."[2]

This tiny word doesn't seem substantial, much less holy. But yes contains transformative power—even more than the omnipotent no.

It's scary to say *yes*. It's risky to say *yes*. It's costly to say *yes*. And as Christians we are taught to say *no* to a lot of choices. But speaking the *y* word with conviction and hope is one of the most Christlike things we can do.

The apostle Paul makes the most direct connection between Jesus and speaking *yes*.

He started the church in Corinth and had spent time there with the community. When he left, he promised that he would be back soon, but a series of events kept Paul from returning as planned.

Paul was like a lot of us. He sometimes overpromised and underdelivered. Life happened to him, and suddenly, despite the best intentions and perhaps without even realizing it, Paul's *yes* morphed into a *no*. He would not return to Corinth after all.

Paul's failure to follow through raised some questions for the Corinthians. If Paul couldn't be trusted with travel plans, how could he be trusted with the gospel? If they couldn't believe his promises, should they believe his proclamations?

In anticipation of these questions, Paul wrote one of the most curious phrases in the New Testament: "In [Jesus], it is always *yes*."[3]

This is where the story of Jesus gets wrapped up in the story of God and God's people. Like Paul, God made a lot of promises over the years. God had promised to make the chosen people fruitful, to bless all nations through them, to establish a peaceful homeland for them, and to deliver them from injustice.

There's a difference between God and human beings like Paul and like us. God always delivers. God always says "yes" and sticks by it. Jesus was God's living, breathing, walking, Yes-in-the-Flesh. No matter what God asked, Jesus nodded. Thumbs up. Full speed ahead. Aye, aye, captain.

For most of us, when we feel a God-nudge or when we catch a whiff of our callings, our first impulse is not acceptance, but analyzing. *Really, God? Is this really best for me? I could stop and help that person, but I need to pick up my dry cleaning.*

People who, like me, gravitate toward *no* must ask which kind of story they are going to live. If we say no enough times, we may find ourselves with a life marked by regret. Or we can live into the story of Christ—one in which we readily say yes to God as we're beckoned into the life we were meant to live.

Being a God-speaker means shouting "Yes!" when the rejection letter arrives, when you want to quit trying, when you're so tired you can't move, when no one is grateful for all you've done, when your critics flay you online. It means climbing out of bed and giving yourself permission to say *yes . . . Yes . . . YES!*

As a writing coach, I operate by a simple mantra: "The answer is always *yes.*" This means living wide-eyed and open-handed for new adventures. The yes life requires us to be expectant and willing to do that which scares us. This means searching for new adventures and being open to adventures finding us. The yes life creates space for God to surprise us and work miracles.[4]

Equally important is realizing that a life of yes doesn't mean throwing out all your routines or being impulsive, traveling whichever direction the wind is blowing. It doesn't mean that our lives are lived according to others' expectations or that we lack healthy boundaries.

As Father Richard Rohr says, "Once you've learned to say a fundamental yes, later nos can be helpful and even necessary: without them, you have no protected boundaries or identity. Our world has coined a term for people who cannot say no: codependents. No one taught them how and when to protect themselves with a necessary no and that a no can be just as sacred as a yes."[5]

Our lives should be so open to God that our first impulse is sacred yes, but we are also meant to be so grounded in wisdom that we know when to speak a "necessary no."[6]

———————

By the age of eighty-seven, Methodist preacher and writer E. Stanley Jones had penned a stack of books and preached an estimated sixty thousand sermons. Then he had a stroke. Jones was left crippled, could barely see, lost the use of one arm, and struggled to talk. From a medical perspective, this was the beginning of the end of his life.

But Jones wasn't ready to give up. Not just yet. He called his daughter to his bedside and whispered: "Daughter, I cannot die now. I have to live to complete another book."

He gained enough strength to speak and dictated his book into a tape recorder. He lived fourteen more months, enough time to complete his final manuscript. Based on Paul's letter to the Corinthians, the book had a three-word title: *The Divine 'Yes.'*

In my effort to explore the word *yes*, I ordered a tattered copy of Jones's work. The writing begins with these words: "Jesus is the Yes—the divine Yes. A great many people today would like to choose Christianity, but they think it is a No to living."[7]

The rest of the book urges people to listen for the voice of God and to be sensitive to the nudges of God. And when we encounter these things to speak a resounding *yes*.

I had no idea Zach's *no* all those years ago would become part of what ushered me into a world of yes. Sometimes nos are God's wondrous gifts that push us toward the greater yes awaiting us.

Saying *yes* offers a first and crucial step toward learning to speak God from scratch. To revive the vocabulary of faith, we must be willing to step out, take risks, and endure setbacks. The great call of God-speakers is learning to say, *yes, yes, yes* no matter the path, until our races are over.

8

Creed: Heresy Hunters and Twitter Farewells

When I first moved to New York City, I was religiously exhausted. I'd spent several years working in and consulting with megachurches. I felt burnt out, unable to enjoy a Sunday service without critiquing every variant decibel and miscued sermon slide. I now hunted for the opposite type of congregation—the kind that meets in a cathedral, burns candles, embraces the word *sacrament*, appreciates liturgy.

I found that kind of church just a few months after arriving. It had everything on my checklist, with one unexpected addition: they often recited creeds.

I believe in God, the Father almighty,

Creator of heaven and earth.

I believe in Jesus Christ, his only Son, our Lord . . .

The first time I said these words out loud, joined by a chorus of fellow God-speakers in an old Lutheran chapel on Twenty-Second Street, the syllables felt strange. Like walking around the house in my grandfather's penny loafers.

Raised as a low-church evangelical, *creed* felt like a dirty word. It sounded like a ritual, and evangelicals often steer clear of anything ritualistic.

The absence of the creeds didn't seem like a loss to me at the time. After all, the historic creeds in their precise wording and order can't be found in the Bible. Though I had practiced informal rituals that weren't in the Bible in previous churches, something about reciting a creed just seemed unnecessary, like speaking Martian.

Over time, however, something shifted in me. A warmth would fall on me halfway through the recitation, and I'd smile hearing my voice intertwine with others. Before long, I looked forward to the weekly discipline and recognized its value. The lines no longer felt rote or rehearsed, but comfortable and familiar. It was like eating breakfast each morning, where you derive energy from an event that, on the surface, seems unspectacular.

Creeds are both expressive and formative. They provide rich summations of what lies at the core of the Christian faith and who Christians have long believed God to be. They remind us of the catholic (meaning "universal") nature of the church—of all those who declare Jesus as God's only Son, conceived by the Holy Spirit, and born of the Virgin Mary—and perhaps never before have we so needed to be reminded that we are linked with millions around the globe. The creeds anchor us in the historic faith, guarding against the temptation to move the goalposts based on which direction culture seems to be advancing. In this way, the creeds provide both a time-tested method of discipleship and a historic guardrail.

The creeds express who God is, what God is like, and how God saves. They largely avoid theological pet peeves at issue today, which have given rise to heresy hunting. A list of topics not included in the creeds:

- The role of women in the church or society
- The nature of sexual orientation or expression
- The existence of hell and who ends up there
- How to read the Bible or understand its special nature
- How you should vote in elections

These important matters are worthy of attention and discussion, but the creeds remind us that we can agree to disagree with other Christians about them.

A phrase comes to mind: "Farewell Rob Bell." These three words were tweeted by pastor John Piper in response to a promo video for then-pastor Rob Bell's forthcoming book *Love Wins: A Book About Heaven, Hell, and the Fate of Every Person Who Ever Lived.*

In the two minute and fifty-eight second clip, Bell seemed to question traditional notions about the existence of a literal, eternal hell. He didn't make many definitive statements, but he leaned hard against sacred cows. That was enough to provoke a harsh response from a stalwart conservative pastor. Though he had never actually read the book in question, Piper bid Bell a blunt *adieu.*

Because of Piper's vast influence among conservative Christians, particularly Calvinists, within hours, protests erupted across social media and Bell was branded with a toxic label: heretic.

The word for "heresy" in Greek translates "choice." Originally, the word was benign and referred to a choice to join a different school of thought. As it turns out, these two words are intertwined. We cannot learn to speak one unless we learn to speak the other as well.

When "heresy" was passed into Latin, early Christian writers used it to mean the choice to accept an "unorthodox sect or doctrine."[1] This new definition stuck, and today, heresy is commonly understood as "a belief or opinion contrary to orthodox religious doctrine."[2]

Centuries ago, heresy was an official, even legal, charge. Those accused of believing or teaching controversial ideas were often tried by ecclesial courts. If found guilty, they were exiled to a remote place or jailed or even set on fire in the town square.

William Tyndale, one of the first to translate the Bible into English, was burned for heresy in the sixteenth-century. (Today, Tyndale is regarded as a hero of the Christian faith.)

Galileo was investigated by the Roman Inquisition for his belief that the earth revolved around the sun (in case you forgot, it does). He recanted that view and avoided the barbeque, but he spent the remainder of his life under house arrest.

From 1450 to 1750 in central Europe, tens of thousands of Christians were executed by their own communities for witchcraft. Three-quarters were widows over fifty years of age.[3] Many Christians believed that "the weaker sex" were more susceptible than males to heretical views and pagan practices.

Our sordid history of heresy hunting should make Christians more cautious about labeling others as heretics. But then again, we Christians are often slow learners.[4]

Compared to their witch-burning ancestors, modern heresy hunters appear more civilized. While the physical stockades have disappeared, you might endure public ridicule from blogs that are solely dedicated to rounding up dissenters. While religious leaders can no longer force "heretics" to stand trial in a court of law, the accused may get kicked out of a pastorate, be shunned by their church community, or "farewelled" on social media.

———————

My friend Cory was once a popular evangelist who traveled across the Southeast speaking at youth ministry events. Thousands of kids flocked to hear his energetic sermons. One day, Cory made the mistake of referencing a controversial author in one of his talks. When he stepped off the stage, the event organizers pulled him aside and informed him that he was now blacklisted from speaking at their events because he had quoted a "heretic." These leaders were quick to spread the word, and soon, Cory was plunged into financial uncertainty.

If heresy hunters come after you today, watch your back. In the internet age, anyone can play judge, jury, and executioner before an infinite audience.

Someone first called me a heretic when I was a twenty-seven-year-old seminary student. I had launched an initiative calling for better steward-ship of the environment. Because I didn't want poor people in developing nations to pay the price of lavish lifestyles, apparently I was "worshiping the creation instead of the Creator."

Two years later, I wrote an exposé on the Religious Right and the rampant partisanship in many churches. Again, dubbed a heretic. Since then, I've penned columns on various issues and had the epithet thrown my way.

Unfortunately, avoiding the heretic label these days is not easy because no universal standard for heresy exists (nor has it ever). Sometimes the criteria presents as political or theological; other times it's mainly cultural. Many say that heresy is anything that denies "the truth of the Bible," but that statement just leads back to an individualistic definition, since there are as many interpretations of "the truth of the Bible" as there are chapters and verses.

The list of heresies varies whether you're Catholic or Protestant, and across denominational, church, and individual lines. Racial divides exist too—black Christians' lists of heresies differ from those of white Christians, for example.[5]

Today, many use the term to describe any belief that doesn't conform to their particular version of Christianity.[6] Ergo, almost anything can fall under this damaging label. Some consider allowing women to serve in church leadership as heresy, while others say denying women's equality is grounds for schism.[7] Others may drop the H-bomb on you if you speak in tongues or have a different perspective about the afterlife.

When theologian Alister McGrath wrote a history of heresy, pastor Rick Warren penned the foreword.[8] The irony? Warren himself has been accused of heresy, for, among other reasons, saying that God can speak to people through dreams.

That's where creeds help. They ground us in our true identities as children of God who can lovingly disagree on most matters. By learning to speak the creeds again, we end the brutal heresy hunt that now runs rampant without restraint or criteria.

The creeds ground us in our true identities as children of God who can lovingly disagree on most matters. By learning to speak the creeds again, we end the brutal heresy-hunt that now runs rampant without restraint or criteria.

We aren't the first to wrestle with the boundaries of faith. As various religious sects arose among early Christians, leaders debated which beliefs should unite those who followed the Jesus way. They drafted creeds, which early Christians recited whenever they gathered. Some may have doubted the words they spoke, but they spoke them anyway, trusting that they were being formed by these declarations.

The historic creeds form an extraordinary baseline for understanding the heart of our faith and what has always made a Christian a "Christian." Whenever believers have added to them and formulated their own lists, the results ranged from slander to murder. Even in periods of disagreement about how to live or interpret the Bible, believers could look to the creeds as a basic formulation of faith's fundamentals.

As conservative theologian Justin Holcomb says, "If a believer genuinely accepts the Nicene Creed, they should not be dubbed a heretic."[9]

The God of the creeds, is unchangeable, but we must remember that the criteria for heresy have evolved throughout history. Some early Christians believed refusing to be circumcised was heresy. In a blink, insisting on circumcision was considered the unorthodox view instead.[10] Believing that all races were equal might have earned you a farewell a half century ago. Today, the situation is reversed. Every Protestant today would have been considered a heretic by much of Christendom just six hundred years ago, prior to the Reformation.

Yesterday's heretics often become today's role models. Christian leaders from Martin Luther to Martin Luther King Jr. were called heretics. And Jesus wasn't crucified for being an orthodox rabbi who always colored inside the lines. He was executed for heresy, and you would be hard-pressed to find an influential religious leader in his time who disagreed with that verdict. Not every false teaching should be called heresy, and not every "heresy" turns out to be a false teaching.

German theologian Helmut Thielicke once said that a person who "speaks to this hour's need" will skirt the edge of heresy. But, he adds, "Only those who risks heresies can gain the truth."[11] His words are as true as ever.

Learning to speak God from scratch is not for the fainthearted. We state what we believe but not always what we ought to say. We use grown-up words but not always the words we used growing up. We speak in ways that are pleasing to the imagination but not always to the establishment.

This means you must be willing to endure name calling and character-assassination attempts.

So even if someone "farewells" you online or labels you a "heretic," inhale deeply and breathe out the words your ancestors have repeated for centuries. History will sort out the rest.

9

Prayer: Folded Hands and Brain Scans

After choosing a church, I decided to settle in and immerse myself in the swirling orbitals of activities, volunteering, and educational classes. I helped organize the annual Easter egg hunt, worked with an organization that provides for homeless people living with HIV/AIDS, served as a volunteer security guard, and joined a Bible study group.

But it was my new pastor, AJ, who triggered transformation in my life by taking me under his wing with lunches and dinners and coffees and cookouts. Each visit was filled with honest conversations, which challenged me to think differently about God, life, and church. And I often left with a good theological book recommendation.

In some ways, it was the first time in my life I'd ever been truly pastored. For most of my existence, I had spent time in my dad's church, both as a congregant and as a staff member. No slight to him—he is the kind of pastor whose rhythms of ministerial self-giving have stoked hope in the embers of what the church should be—but your parent can never fully pastor you. No matter how much time is invested in ministering and mentoring, your parent will be your parent first, and not your pastor.

After a few months of pouring himself into my spiritual development, AJ invited me to join him on retreat at Holy Cross, a modest Anglican monastery upstate near Poughkeepsie. Something of a mystic, he planned the retreat to include time discussing the work of the late Catholic teacher Henri Nouwen and contemplative practices, such as silence and solitude.

The second day of retreat, we gathered in a musty room on the second floor of the creaky monastery, and AJ explained a way of praying that was different from what I was used to.

Lectio divina is a fancy Latin term that means "divine reading." To engage, you read a scripture in repetition while allowing the words to wash over you. Each time the passage moves from breath to air, listeners focus on the syllables and select a single sacred word that sticks in their minds. This word becomes a point of focus, quieting the inner noise and attuning us to divine presence.[1]

Western Christians have always valued prayer, so the seriousness and intentionality of lectio divina is not as jarring as the way it postures your spirit. It is less about giving and getting, and more about being. Less about speaking and more about listening. These shifts are unique for many Western Christians like me who are used to spending "prayer time" begging God to give them what they want or to act when God feels absent.

Prayer is simple, my Sunday school teacher once told me. Just remember four letters: ACTS. More than an acronym, these letters were a recipe simple enough to whip up in any life stage and in the face of any struggle.

- *A* stands for "adoration." This is the opening act where you express your love for God and offer praise.
- *C* represents "confession." This is where you put yourself in your place and talk about your terrible sins.
- *T* means "thanksgiving." This swings the spotlight right back to God. You offer gratitude for the good gifts in your life—food, family, friends, and whatever else comes to mind.
- *S* is for "supplication." This is really just a fancy synonym for requests. It goes last, of course, because you don't want to sound greedy. The first three stages are to soften up God for the grocery list you pull out of your pocket in the finale. Amen and amen, am I right?

I prayed this way for years, and though formulaic, the pattern worked well enough. I never forgot the four steps, and by the time I was a teenager, I could run through them without hesitance.

I don't know how many spiritual seekers use this formula, but many Western Christians pray with the same basic assumptions that prayer serves two main purposes: giving something to God (adoration and thanks) and getting something from God (forgiveness following confession and answers to your requests). This way of understanding prayer makes sense to those who live in capitalistic America, in part, because it's transactional—all about giving and getting.

The day I first engaged lectio divina, however, I encountered a new way of understanding the word *prayer* and those who use the tool for spiritual formation. The practice was relational, rather than transactional, which is how it becomes transformational.

Interestingly, this way of praying can be understood in terms of both spirituality and science. Dr. Andrew Newberg is a neuroscientist who is fascinated by questions concerning the universe, meaning, existence, God, and spiritual practice. His research team has conducted brain scans of people engaged in various intercessory acts—from Franciscan nuns reciting prayers to Tibetan Buddhists in meditation, from chanting Sikhs to Pentecostal Christians talking to God in tongues. The findings are changing the way we understand these disciplines.

Newberg's subjects are injected with a radioactive tracer and scanned using either MRI or SPECT imaging. Every subject's brain is scanned twice: once in a resting state and again while engaged in the spiritual practice. The data shows links between these practices and changes in brain activity.

When subjects were praying or meditating, for example, their ability to concentrate increased dramatically. Brain function sharpened, and the subjects became hyperfocused and aware. When some subjects talked in tongues, the activity of the frontal lobes decreased rather than increased. Researchers say that this seems to support the idea that they are not purposefully doing it but rather allowing it to happen to them.

Often, those performing prayerful disciplines reported experiencing an intense loss of self. Low chanting, worshipful melodies, and whispered prayer, for example, all turn on the hippocampus directly and block neuronal traffic to other brain regions. The result, he says, is a "softening of the boundaries of the self" that opens the door to a greater sense of spiritual connection with God.[2]

The studies also compared the way one felt when being engaged in spiritual practices. If a subject described feeling the love of God during a religious practice, the part of the brain that helps us feel love was often activated. If a subject experienced a restfulness, the part of the brain that helps us feel secure was often activated.

"We've found that religious and spiritual practices have a profound impact on us. If you visualize in your mind, it activates certain centers in the brain. If you engage in prayer, you'll activate other centers in the brain," Newberg says. "And we don't just see immediate variations in activity. Our studies are starting to show that we can fundamentally change the brain through religious experience."[3]

Not only does prayer change our brains and bodies in the moment, but when practiced over time, it leads to permanent physiological transformation.

In one study conducted, Newberg focused on subjects who had experienced memory loss and trained them in a simple meditation practice. They then engaged in this practice for twelve minutes a day over an eight-week period. Results showed that the subjects' frontal lobes and thalamus were more active not just while they were meditating but also at rest. In short, subjects experienced long-term increases in cognitive function and cerebral blood flow.

"If these people who have never really done a practice before can affect this kind of change in a short period of time doing such a practice," Newberg says, "you can imagine what is happening in the brain of a nun who is engaged in prayer for hours a day over fifty years. It is changing the way her brain works and even the way she looks at reality."[4]

> **Not only does prayer change our brains and bodies in the moment, but when practiced over time, it leads to permanent physiological transformation.**

If spiritual practices provide a general strengthener for the brain, he notes, the effects could spill over into many other areas of life. A person who engages in spiritual practices might be better able to find his way home if he gets lost or work better at his job. Spiritual practices may even indirectly improve a person's golf game.

The Christian tradition maintains that the physical world often reveals spiritual truth. The psalmist often connects God's handiwork to divine knowledge. The opening chapter of Romans says, "For since the creation of the world God's invisible qualities—his eternal power and divine nature—have been clearly seen, being understood from what has been made, so that people are without excuse."[5]

Science and nature often point us toward the supernatural. When we pay attention, we may uncover information that helps us understand God and may even help us reimagine prayer.

In Romans 12:1–2, Paul urges readers to "offer your *bodies* as a living sacrifice" and "be transformed by the renewing of your *mind*." Could it be that our brains are designed to help us love God more and better as we connect with God through prayer?

Western and Eastern Christians remind us that prayer may be used for giving to God, receiving from God, being in the presence of God, or hearing the voice of God.

Prayer, though, is also about transformation. Our practices should make us better, stronger, happier, and healthier by strengthening our concentration, fortifying our memory, and changing the way we think.

Amen.

10

Pain: Chronic Conditions and Other Metaphors

On my journey to speak God from scratch, I chose some words. But other words chose me. The word *pain* entered my life without warning on a gray December morning when I woke up and could not feel my hands.

Springing from my bed, I wrung out my arms hoping the sensation would return. I shook them violently to no avail. Rushing to the bathroom, I held them under hot water. Then frigid water. Neither helped. Anxiety seized me. The previous day, the doctor's office had left a voice mail about coming in to discuss results of my recent blood work.

I phoned my physician right away. Two days later I sat on her examination table, my hands still numb. Blood work indicated slightly elevated cholesterol levels unconnected to my symptoms. Everything else seemed normal. The doctor shrugged and diagnosed me with "probably carpal tunnel syndrome." She suggested I see a hand surgeon.

I visited my parents in Atlanta the following week and waited on scheduling with the surgeon. I assumed my body would bounce back. It always had before. For more than thirty years, every scratch and sore and ache and injury had healed. This time, it did not.

Within days, prickly tingles crept up my arm and spread to my shoulders. The numbness turned into pain that burned, ached, and stabbed. Even my fingernails throbbed. I bypassed the hand surgeon and visited a neurologist instead. He performed tests using electrified needles inserted into my muscles and shock pads placed on the skin. This wasn't carpal tunnel syndrome, he concluded.

Next came a series of tests for minor problems like vitamin deficiencies, major illnesses like Lupus, and life-threatening conditions like multiple myeloma. Each brought excruciating waiting and worry. I was, after all, a writer whose livelihood depended on having control of his hands.

After a series of scans, my neurologist passed me to a colleague who repeated previous tests and conducted new ones. All were negative. Referral after referral led me to the offices of six different neurologists. When nothing changed, I hit the Eject button.

My symptom list grew with each passing month. First came nerve twitches in my legs, arms, back, and face. Then a paradox of sapping fatigue and insomnia. Severe panic attacks struck without warning, and I broke out in excruciating shingles from the overwhelming stress. The slightest stressor—a large crowd or a long line, common in this city—left me exhausted and bedridden.

One night I confessed to a roommate that I wanted to run into the street and tear my skin off. My roommate sat next to me while I slept clutching a stuffed bunny for comfort.

I grasped for anyone who would help, scheduling appointments with cardiologists and chiropractors, naturopaths and nutritionists, holistic doctors and Hasidic Jewish healers.

The revolving door of physicians left me without a diagnosis and drowning in an ocean of medications: anti-inflammatory drugs, muscle relaxants, nerve pills, pain killers, antiepileptic drugs, sleeping pills, and a healthy dose of Lexapro and Xanax to keep me from freaking out.

My life blurred. My ability to work was reduced to a meager three hours a day. My social life disintegrated, leaving me in depths of loneliness I'd never known before. Everything familiar looked strange. Pain tormented me at every moment. I awoke to pain, worked with pain, dined with pain, and fought for sleep despite pain's presence.

I was helpless like Job, brought low before God out of sheer desperation. When he was faced with his own pain, he could only bow before the Divine and listen to the wind. The difference between us is that once Job submitted, God restored him. I had no such luck. I was incarcerated in the prison of my own body.

While the swiftness of my breakdown confused me, the isolation it brought crushed me. Without physical manifestations of my illness, even those closest to me failed to grasp the severity of my struggle. But that didn't stop them from trying to offer a quick fix.

One friend said she heard about a special tea that would cure illness like this in a jiffy. (It didn't.) Others suggested it was my meat consumption or some kind of dietary issue. (It wasn't.) I increased time spent with my counselor to try to locate the emotional source of my problem. (Still nothing.)

Beyond a few easy-fix recommendations, most friends weren't interested in much discussion about the matter. The more I talked about it, the less they came around. I had lost my health, and now I was losing my community.

No one can feel what another feels, so only those who live with pain can relate. Healthy people just cannot understand. This makes chronic illness an isolating experience.

I'm a fighter. So I kept seeing doctors and alternative health practitioners, and I continued researching in medical journals. I made up my mind not to give up or give in. More than a year and a half after I woke up with invisible hands, I found a physician who could help me manage my condition. I still have pain most days, but I am able to work and think with clarity and sleep most nights without popping a pill. This is a better situation than the experience of most people afflicted with chronic pain.

Some sacred words could be deleted from the vocabulary of faith and we would barely notice. Not *pain*. This is a part of life whether you have a chronic physical condition or not. In the Hindu scripture, *The Bhagavad Gita*, the god Krishna calls life "the place of pain." Which is to say, life is something of a chronic pain condition, filled with hurts. No one passes through life without accumulating his or her fair share of scabs and scars.

> In a world where so many are writhing under the weight of chronic pain, we must find a way to speak about pain that is helpful, informed, and compassionate.

Most pain is temporary, of course. The body has a remarkable way of fixing itself. Chronic pain, however, is the kind that doesn't heal over time. It drags, persists, and often worsens. The dramatic rise in this sort of pain forces us to be more precise and thoughtful in the way we understand and use this word.

More than 100 million Americans struggle with chronic pain—from piercing headaches to a throbbing lower back to mysterious body aches. Those who struggle with chronic pain report higher levels of mental health struggles than those who do not. More than half say the pain affects their sleep, concentration, work, and enjoyment of life. Chronic pain is so miserable that one-third of the afflicted say they would spend every penny they have if it would relieve their pain. The problem is so vast that it has now reached crisis levels, costing society as much as $635 billion annually (that's $2,000 per American per year).[1]

In a world where so many are writhing under the weight of chronic pain, Americans—and especially Jesus followers—must find a way to speak about pain that is helpful, informed, and compassionate. On my pain journey, I realized that pain is often talked about in two opposite ways. Both are incomplete and often heap more hurt on the afflicted.

Some religious traditions treat pain—physical, emotional, or mental—as an unmitigated tragedy. They may even suggest a person's sins or faithlessness as the root cause. If we get rid of the sin or increase our faith, the pain will vanish. This framework is harmful in part because it heaps guilt on the pained. People see themselves as the cause of their pain or the reason it isn't resolving, and sometimes seek out spiritual solutions to pain at the exclusion of medical remedies.

Other religious traditions speak of pain in the opposite way—as a gift—a primary portal through which we encounter the Divine. Some ascetic and monastic traditions resist the temptation to escape pain and even seek out discomfort. The goal is to embrace pain. This framework is harmful because the pained do not experience their pain as a positive force, and telling them it is so feels cruel.

Between these two poles, a third way understands pain as a negative and unfortunate presence that has the ability to grow us, teach us, and even lead us into greater spiritual awareness. We can seek to cure pain while also collaborating with pain. To sit with pain and listen to pain, even while we try to alleviate it.

———————

At the lowest point in my pain journey, I found myself in a pharmacy waiting area with a close Christian friend. Feeling philosophical, she asked whether I believed my pain could be caused by the devil or perhaps was sent by God for some greater purpose. I told her that I didn't think those were the only possibilities.

"All I know is that pain is a teacher," I said, "but I do not know where he was educated."

Rather than speak of pain as the enemy of all enemies or a celebrated house guest, we might talk of pain as an unfortunate, terrible teacher. We desire to opt out of his class, but somehow we keep finding ourselves sitting before him. As long as we are present, we might as well learn something.

On my own pain journey, I've begun pausing to reflect. To listen to the lessons pain is trying to teach.

I've learned that I am not omnipotent and must relinquish control of my present as well as my future.

I've realized that I am not infinite, and I should enjoy each day without rushing through.

I've learned that I'm not empathetic, and I now find myself more attentive to painful cries around me.

I've also stopped taking any pain-free moments for granted. Gratitude is now a greater part of my life rhythm.

Carl Jung once said, if you kill your pain before you answer its questions, you kill yourself along with it. If I could take a magic pill and rid myself of the burning nerves and aching muscles and elevated anxiety once-and-for-all, I would. If possible, I bet you'd end whatever pain you might be experiencing—a health condition, an emotional devastation, or any great misfortune. I do not believe God wants suffering for us.

But as long as the pain is here, we might as well answer the questions it is raising. And in so doing, we come to know God, others, and ourselves more intimately.

11

Disappointment: Dopamine Roller Coasters and Palm Branches

My chronic pain journey was also a voyage of disappointment.

I was saddened by friends who seemed largely uncompassionate. Without open wounds or unsightly scars, a wheelchair or a cast, I seemed fine to onlookers. As a result, people tended to ignore or even dismiss my suffering. Some told me that I was probably just stressed out and working too hard. If I could learn to relax, then my suffering would subside. Since this framed the condition as self-inflicted, it added guilt to my misery. Other friends suggested it was "all in my head" or the result of depression and anxiety. That made me feel crazy in addition to tormented.

One of my closest friends, who was particularly callous, told me that I just texted too much and the impact of my fingers pressing the screen on my smartphone was impacting my nerves. If I would just be more present at dinners, the pain would subside. When I tried his protocol and it failed, he jokingly asked whether I might be a hypochondriac. This kind of wound doesn't heal.

My disappointment with others ached, but it was nothing compared to what I felt toward God.

Come on, God. You know my story. You were there when my neighbor abused me as a child. You know how awkward and alienated I felt dur-

ing adolescence. You know how I've struggled with anxiety and depression my entire adult life. I'm starting to see sunlight, to get a little relief, and then this happens? Really?

This is the edited version. I spoke words to God that the MPAA would bar from a PG-13 movie.

On November 9, 2016, *New York* magazine published an article on the science of disappointment. The article opened by stating the obvious, which is that "the feeling of being let down is actually one of life's toughest emotional experiences."[1]

Of course, most people don't need a *New York* writer to know that this is true, that disappointment hurts.

A spouse or partner, that person who made butterflies dance inside you, cheated on you and then hid it.

Your colleague smeared you in a meeting to steal the promotion you earned.

The child you prayed over since birth stormed out of the house swearing to never return.

A forgotten birthday, a withheld apology, a bucketful of lies from someone you'd die for.

Disappointment is an unavoidable part of being human, but as the *New York* article noted, the experience is physiological, not just emotional. The feeling of disappointment is linked to your levels of dopamine, the brain's "pleasure" chemical, released during positive life experiences. The dopamine systems in your brain do not just react to what you experience; they attempt to *predict* what you want or need.

Here's how it works: Your brain generates expectations about the future. Often these expectations are based on what you want.

Something you perceive as good has happened in the past, so you begin to predict it will happen in the future. Before it even happens, your dopamine levels begin to rise in response to your *expectations*. You feel the rush of anticipation. Then, when that good thing actually occurs, you get a double shot of dopamine.

Here's the rub: Life doesn't always give us what we expect. People fail us. People hurt us. People lay us on the altars of their own selfishness. When you *don't* get the desired result—you experience what researchers call a "reward-prediction error"—not only do your dopamine levels fall, they plummet from the heightened level generated by your expectations.

Now, instead of receiving a double shot of dopamine, you receive none. You crash doubly hard. "Not only do you *not* get what you wanted, but you also feel the displeasure of having been wrong." The point? "Losing hurts even worse . . . when it's not what you were expecting."[2]

In the valley of my disappointment, I discovered a gospel story that's a portrait of what a reward-prediction error looks like en masse. It tells of one of the most significant dopamine rises—leading to a historic crash. All four Gospel writers included the narrative, with their own twist. [3]

Dust was swirling across the scorching desert as a rebel Rabbi and his band of coconspirators climbed up to Jerusalem.[4] Rather than slip into the city unannounced, Jesus did something strange. He told a couple of his disciples to go to a particular place and retrieve a donkey for him to ride into the city.

The rebel Jesus turned his face toward a city that kills prophets, stones truth-tellers, and executes troublemakers. With a deep sigh, he steeled himself, mounted the humble beast, and *clip-clopped* toward the Kidron Valley.

When the Jerusalemites saw Jesus approaching, they erupted in excitement. They began stripping off their cloaks and spreading them across the road. The crowd whacked branches off trees and laid them across Jesus' path.

If this weren't enough pomp and ceremony, the crowd broke into a Passover song. Matthew told us the procession turned the whole city into "turmoil." The Greek word is the root for the English word *seismic*. The city trembled as Jesus approached.

The story begins with great expectations, which are easy to miss. Jesus has just been in Bethany, close to Jerusalem, where he resurrected his friend Lazarus from the dead. Lazarus's eyes have barely adjusted to the sunlight and his story has spread throughout the region. Hearing this story, the crowds react, their brains bathed in dopamine. They begin to predict how God will act in their lives based on the way God acted before.

With Lazarus, Jesus encountered a man who died before his time, and he chose to intervene, reviving his friend from death. It's only natural that the people began to expect that, in the case of their occupied city, Jesus will intervene again. He will work a miracle. He will expel the occupiers and resurrect God's people in God's city. Expectations formed and anticipation rose.

The palm branches signaled the crowd's high expectations, a symbol largely lost on those of us who are separated from the culture and chronology of the story. Jewish history told of a man named Judas Maccabaeus, a freedom fighter who entered Jerusalem two hundred years prior to Jesus. As he approached, people waved palm branches and sang hymns. When Judas finally arrived, he defeated the Syrian king, recaptured the temple, expelled the pagans, and reigned for a century before the Romans recaptured the city.

God saved them from an occupier once before when an uncommon man trotted into town. With a new sheriff on the horizon, they began to predict another takeover was about to happen.

Their song declared, "Hosanna to the Son of David! Blessed is he who comes in the name of the Lord!"

This is a song that Jews sang at the beginning of Passover. It's taken from Psalm 118, the psalm most quoted by the New Testament. If you read the whole thing, it tells of an enemy swarming like bees driving the psalmist to the brink of destruction. Then, God sweeps in with a mighty hand and wipes out the enemy. The word *hosanna* means, "Lord, save now." They are asking Jesus to drive out the enemy army and restore order.

Even the donkey plays a role in elevating expectations, drawing an image from Zechariah 9:9, a prophetic passage that many of these Jerusalemites would have heard before. "See, your king comes to you, righteous and victorious, lowly and riding on a donkey."

That night around dinner tables across Jerusalem, Jews discussed the day in hushed voices. "Could this be the king we've been waiting for? He was riding a donkey, after all." By the time Jesus mounted that donkey and descended into town, their dopamine systems are in overdrive.

The scene created by the crowds demonstrates how assumptions about who God is lead to expectations about how God works.

We can't fault them for harboring these expectations. They weren't baseless, after all. Psalm 118 *does* talk about God destroying our enemies. But it begins by saying, "Give thanks to the LORD, for he is good. His love endures forever." We celebrate and welcome God, therefore, because God is good and loving and kind. Not because God will vanquish our foes. By selective reading, the people of Jerusalem have ignored the greater context.

Zechariah 9:9 mentions the Messiah King riding into town on a donkey. But the next verse says,

> I will take away the chariots from Ephraim
> and the warhorses from Jerusalem,
> and the battle bow will be broken.
> He will proclaim peace to the nations. (verse 10)

This Messiah wasn't coming to ignite war, orchestrate a coup, or pick a fight. This Messiah was coming to bring peace, to rid the land of weapons rather than use them for violence.

The Jerusalemites aren't much different from us. I've spent my whole life in churches—evangelical and mainline, small and mega, liturgical congregations and those with ear-splitting rock bands. I can't think of one that hasn't projected expectations onto God.

Most pick an image of God that best suits their desires, stoking these expectations among their congregants. Which is why the expectations you place on God are almost always the result of which religious context has most shaped you.

Maybe you expect God to be a heavenly bellhop whose job is to satisfy your deepest desires. Or perhaps God is a holy matchmaker who will secure a spouse for you. Maybe God is a cosmic bodyguard who will protect you from harm. Or the world's best nanny who will make sure your children turn out right. Maybe your God is the divine doctor who will heal your every physical and mental ailment. Or perhaps your God is a wonder-working accountant who will solve all your financial problems—provided you drop off a portion in the church coffers, of course.

Humans tend to assume that God is the deity they want. All you have to do is snatch up a couple of verses that seem to support this version of God. You know, write them on an index card and post them on your bathroom mirror. Then you spend a few years listening to a pastor reinforce them through selective storytelling. Before you know it, the cement of those assumptions dries and you begin expecting God to work in particular ways in your life. Not unlike the people of Jerusalem.

Our frameworks of expectations work pretty well for us . . . as long as God seems to do what we want God to do. But the moment God doesn't conform to our expectations, our whole world rattles.

A baby is born with a disability.

A person you love abandons you for another.

A friend dies before her time.

The expectations you placed on God ferment into distrust, into disappointment. As author Anne Lamott says, "Expectations are resentments under construction."

On September 19, 2015, Seth Stephens-Davidowitz wrote an article in the *New York Times* Sunday Review titled "Googling for God." The idea behind the article is that Google search data can tell us a lot about the psychology of the modern age. When it comes to God, many people won't share their struggles with their faith leaders or friends, but they type them into Google where they can ask with both impunity and anonymity.

Stephens-Davidowitz sifted through a decade's worth of Google searches and found the most searched questions about God:

Why does God allow suffering?
Why does God need so much praise?
Why does God hate me?
Why did God make me ugly?
Why did God make me gay?
Why did God make me black?

I noticed a common thread binding each of these questions together: disappointment with God.

Many of us—perhaps tens of millions—have a common experience when it comes to spirituality. We expect God to *be* something and then discover that God is not at all like that. Or we expect God to *do* something only to realize that God seems to be preoccupied with other matters.

In these moments, a tsunami of disappointment crashes down on us, wrecking the constructions of faith from the beachhead of our lives.

C. S. Lewis's conclusion to the question of suffering in *The Problem of Pain* was that "God whispers to us in our pleasures, speaks in our conscience, but shouts in our pain: It is His megaphone to rouse a deaf world."[5]

It sounds beautiful, but it's not all that comforting.

Lewis seems to have realized the simplicity of this view later in life. After Lewis's wife died and he penned *A Grief Observed,* he wrote about what it is like to go to God, "When your need is desperate, when all other help is vain, and what do you find? A door slammed in your face, and a sound of bolting and double bolting on the inside. After that, silence. . . . Not that I am (I think) in much danger of ceasing to believe in God. The real danger is of coming to believe such dreadful things about Him. The conclusion I dread is not 'So there's no God after all,' but 'So this is what God's really like. Deceive yourself no longer.'"[6]

Perhaps the greatest threat to faith is not *doubting* God but being *disappointed* with God.

The Palm Sunday story displays the transition from expectation to disappointment in Technicolor. The triumph becomes a trial, and the trial becomes an execution. Jesus entered the city on a donkey, but we know he will leave in a body bag. This is not just a fun parade; Jesus is walking down death row.

Viewing this story with fresh eyes, I felt I was glimpsing a picture of what happens to a group of very religious people when they feel disappointed by God. At the start, the crowds embrace Jesus with dopamine levels soaring and shouts of "Save us now!" As soon as Jesus turns out to be something other than the Savior they expect, their hosannas morph into "Crucify him!"

Jesus is a king but not the kind they wanted. He will serve rather than be served. He will die and not be killed. He enters unarmed, waging peace. This makes a larger point, that God does not intend to meet our *expectations*. Instead, God intends to meet our *needs*.

This type of God makes me uncomfortable. I don't want vegetables when I'm craving candy. I want a God who satisfies my desires, whether or not those align with my needs.

The story begins with expectation and ends with disappointment. The crowd has come to the festival, but they can't stomach the funeral. They join the celebration, but they will not stay for the crucifixion. They are willing to sing, but they will not suffer.

And so it is with us.

We welcome God into our lives with anticipation, with expectation. We're laying down cloaks and waving palm branches with all we've got.

But . . .

then . . .

God turns out to be someone we don't recognize, and we scatter like smoke in the wind.

One of the most interesting features of this story is how much preparation Jesus does. He lines up everything, making sure to trigger the crowd's expectations. It's like Jesus has hired a PR agency, indicating that he knows exactly what he is stirring up.

But why? Is he trying to disappoint them?

No. I think he is trying to disillusion them.

The word *disillusion* has gotten a bad rap in recent times, but it's a gift God gives with abundance.

Disillusionment is, well, the *loss of an illusion*. It is what happens when you take a lie—about the world, about yourself, about those you love, about God—and replace it with the truth. Disillusionment occurs when God shatters our fantasies, tears down our idols, dismantles our cardboard cutouts. It is the result of discovering that God does not conform to our expectations but rather exists as a mystery beyond those expectations.

The definition offered by Episcopal preacher Barbara Brown Taylor may be the best I've seen. She describes disillusionment as the sacred experiences that cut us down to size and remind us of our smallness in this expansive universe. These experiences are often painful, but never bad, because they make us shed the lies we've mistaken for truth: "Disillusioned, we find out what is not true and we are set free to seek what is—if we dare—to turn away from the God who was supposed to be in order to seek the God who is."[7]

When we talk about disappointment, we're really speaking about a divine gateway to spiritual clarity that can only come through a life-shattering experience of disillusionment.

Which is to say, this Gospel story is not about donkeys and palm branches at all. It's a reminder that placing expectations on God based on our wants is a recipe for resentment. But nurturing openness to divine mystery is a framework for faith.

> **Disillusionment occurs when God shatters our fantasies, tears down our idols, dismantles our cardboard cutouts.**

My pain disorder has persisted despite my best efforts, but so has my relationship with God. I refuse to let my disappointment sever divine ties. And you know what? Over time, I've begun to uncover and shed illusions. I'm dismantling mirages I've constructed around productivity and identity and self-worth.

I can no longer work twelve-to-fourteen-hour days, so . . .

I can no longer pretend that who I am is enhanced by how much I produce, so . . .

I can no longer ground my sense of worth in accomplishments and accolades, and . . .

I can no longer pretend that God will keep me healthy or heal my every ache and pain.

I have traded these lies for a truth: that in times of difficulty, God offers us presence, not a parachute. This exchange of falsehood for fact transformed my disappointment into disillusionment. And disillusion turned out to be a horrible, wonderful gift.

What we experience as disappointment is an invitation to give up holding tight to what we hope is true. To stop trying to cast God in our image. To let God be who God is, not who we wish God would be.

The choice is ours. And who knows? If we decide to step off the dopamine roller coaster, maybe we'll find ourselves at the foot of a cross, giving up all we have for the One who gave up everything for us.

12

Mystery: Apologetics, Addictions, and Infinite Knowability

All religious traditions operate with a certain linguistic selectivity. That is, certain sacred terms are spoken in perpetuity, while others barely see the light of day. We all prefer some words and avoid others—a subconscious tendency that is less about grammar than ideology. Sacred terms are signposts pointing to sacred ideas. The more weight that a community places on certain theological ideas, the more often they will utilize the words that point to those ideas.

Growing up evangelical meant we spoke of sin often because our theology was pietistic. We used words like *conversion* and *salvation* a lot because we were evangelistic, and we spoke of hell a lot because we were infernalistic. This makes perfect sense in hindsight. We saw the world primarily as a place where "sinful" people needed to "convert" to Christianity and receive the "salvation" of God to avoid roasting on God's spit in "hell" for all eternity.

These types of words took up disproportionate space in our vocabulary of faith, elbowing other sacred words into retirement. One word I don't remember hearing spoken much was *mystery*.

My community placed a heavy emphasis on apologetics, which is the art of making logical defenses for the Christian faith. The twenty-first century called for a well-reasoned approach, so we were trained in how to intellectually battle non-Christians of every shape and stripe with complex arguments. We made a "case for Christ" and a "case for faith" and a "case for Christianity." We forced people to consider our "evidence that demands a verdict" and proclaimed, "I don't have enough faith to be an atheist." The great depths of God and faith were boiled down to arguments small enough to fit on an index card, easily memorized and ready to deploy in debates.

> A hyperrational approach to faith has pitfalls, including a de-emphasis of *mystery* in our vocabulary and our theological frameworks.

Our emphasis on apologetics was beneficial, since it forced us to identify the tensions and ambiguities of our faith while raising levels of critical thinking. Apologetics even helped us dismantle some of the truly specious arguments made by antireligionists.

A hyperrational approach to faith has pitfalls, including a de-emphasis of *mystery* in our vocabulary and our theological frameworks. For us, *mystery* described a divine puzzle waiting to be solved. With enough facts and argumentation, the unknown could be revealed.

I began to use the word *mystery* more as I grew older, but only as the junk drawer where I placed everything I couldn't explain through logic. If a college professor posed an ethical problem that my framework couldn't solve, that was a *mystery*. If a combative friend used the problem of evil to paint me into the corner, I'd chalk it up to *mystery*.

Using this word was like inserting a shoulder shrug into the conversation, yet somehow it felt justified. I knew that God was bigger than me and beyond me and smarter than me. The problem was, once I labeled something a "mystery," I stopped thinking about it altogether.

In New York, however, I was being drawn away from an apologetic framework into a more mystical framework. I was leaning into ambiguities and tensions and doubts, and it was actually strengthening the resolve of my faith. I began to understand, as Thomas Aquinas once noted, that the highest knowledge of God is to know that we do not know God. In this framework, embracing the mystery of God is the high-water mark of faith.

As life-giving as this shift was for me, my lingering understanding of *mystery* as the "unknowable matters of faith" created a kind of religious cognitive dissonance. Exploring these matters breathed life into my spiritual lungs, and yet the endeavor felt futile. The word in the Bible refers to a secret. If you can't know this secret, why try?

A switch flipped when I spent time with Richard Rohr, a Franciscan friar, in the desert of New Mexico. "What about mystery? Why waste time trying to know something that is unknowable?" I asked him.

The jovial seventy-four-year-old bald man smiled with a glimmer in his eye.

"That's a great question, Jonathan, but I think maybe you misunderstand what mystery is. A mystery is not something that is *unknowable*; it is something that is *infinitely knowable*."

13

God: Tattooed Jesus and a Full-Narrative Deity

Last year my roommate and I hosted a weekly spiritual discussion group in our apartment. We welcomed Christians, Buddhists, Jews, agnostics, and all manner of people with the purpose of exploring big questions about meaning, purpose, transcendence, and love. During one of the first discussions, my friends and I sat in a circle and I asked them to close their eyes. After a brief pause, I spoke a single word: "God." I paused again and then asked them to describe what came to mind when they heard that word.

Together we compared notes, and needless to say, our answers varied widely.

If you want to speak God from scratch, a good first step is pausing to consider what you mean when you speak the word *God* itself. The images and feelings conjured by this word turn out to be a matter of great consequence. As twentieth-century pastor and author A. W. Tozer quipped, "What comes to mind when we think about God is the most important thing about us."

Our understanding of the word *God* shapes the way we relate to God, ourselves, and the billions of others with whom we share life on this round rock. A sweeping survey by Baylor University's Institute for Studies of Religion sorted people's perceptions of God into four categories:

Authoritarian God—High level of anger and high level of
engagement
Critical God—High level of anger and low level of engagement
Distant God—Low level of anger and low level of engagement
Benevolent God—Low level of anger and high level of
engagement

According to the study, the way people perceived God was a more reliable predictor of their values and behavior than any other measurement.[1]

In a separate study conducted by Marymount Manhattan College, the "belief in a punitive God was significantly associated with an increase in social anxiety, paranoia, obsession, and compulsion." Further, the study stated that beliefs in a punitive God "facilitates threat assessments that the world is dangerous and even that God poses a threat of harm, thereby increasing psychiatric symptomatology."[2]

These studies indicate that the way God is perceived can have devastating effects on the God-speakers themselves. When we use our words to speak about a terribly angry God, we often become terribly angry people. If we speak about a God who rules by fear, we become people who live in fear.

You don't have to look far to find examples of vehement Christians preaching the gospel of a punitive deity these days.

Shortly after I moved to New York, for example, the evangelical world witnessed the public downfall of pastor Mark Driscoll. For years, Driscoll was the preacher that Christians loved to hate. He was culturally savvy, and his hip clothes and mannerisms made his hellfire-and-damnation message all the more surprising. His sermons seemed more suited to a traveling sawdust revival than a contemporary megachurch in the progressive city of Seattle.

Driscoll's strong positions earned him a cult-like following in a particular theological camp, and by 2013, he seemed unstoppable. With a little market manipulation, his books hit bestseller lists.[3] He became a sought-after speaker at Christian conferences, shouting his message to thousands of adoring fans. He ran a church-planting network to replicate his brand of theology in congregations around the world, and his multicampus church was exploding.

Christians who didn't love Driscoll loathed him.

At the pinnacle of his popularity in 2013, something about Mark Driscoll unsettled me. He was more than a fundamentalist. He seemed unbridled and unaccountable, with an acquired taste for foot. His raison d'être seemed to be creating conflict with needlessly bombastic statements.

> If you want to speak God from scratch, a good first step is pausing to consider what you mean when you speak the word God itself.

Some of his controversial comments stemmed from his beliefs about gender. He promoted antiquated views of women, saying that females shouldn't hold leadership positions in the church since they are "more gullible and easier to deceive than men" and stating that stay-at-home dads are "worse than unbelievers."[4]

When religious leader Ted Haggard was caught in a scandal involving a male prostitute, Driscoll speculated that perhaps Haggard's wife may be to blame for his infidelity if she had neglected her appearance.[5]

Perhaps his most concerning remarks regarded his conceptions of God. He viewed God as a vengeful, angry, temperamental deity who burned with rage against sinful humans. He once screamed to his congregation,

"God hates you."[6] In my opinion, one of his most stunning quotes was this: "In Revelation, Jesus is a prize-fighter with a tattoo down His leg, a sword in His hand and the commitment to make someone bleed. That is a guy I can worship. I cannot worship the hippie, diaper, halo Christ because I cannot worship a guy I can beat up."[7]

Like a case study for the Marymount and Baylor studies, Driscoll's depiction of God as a temperamental jerk mirrored Driscoll's staff's description of their pastor. Numerous employees quit under duress, claiming he built a culture of fear and abuse. Roughly two dozen former employees leveled charges against him, claiming he "engaged in a pattern of abusive and intimidating conduct and that he has not changed his domineering behavior." He had even posted angry comments to a Christian message board under the pseudonym "William Wallace II."[8] One former pastor said Driscoll was "driven by Narcissism."[9] These allegations eventually contributed to Driscoll's resignation.

Many Christians dismiss Driscoll's comments as hyperbole, but if you drill down, a number of Christians do think of God as a tattooed, tough guy with more than enough wrath to go around.

According to the Baylor study, around 150 million Americans believe in an angry God (authoritarian or critical). That means about half of all Americans talk about God as if God were a stone-fisted ruler. A number of other Christian leaders refer to God in such a way. Christian author Paul Tripp has said, "God is angry, and his anger is relentless." God is so angry, according to Pastor John Piper, that God once sent a deadly tornado to Minneapolis as a "gentle but firm warning" to a particularly progressive-leaning Lutheran denomination.[10]

What kind of deity do you envision when you speak of God?

Many believers, like me, spent much of their lives in religious contexts with a heavy emphasis on the wrath and judgment and righteous anger of

God. God is a macho man who needs anger management. God is an uncompromising and temperamental warrior—a pretty good fella as long as you manage to obey all the rules and stay on God's good side.

Then they read the Bible. Not a flat reading of the text that attempts to harmonize each different author's perspective, but a contextualized reading of the whole story that embraces a view of God that emerges as the biblical narrative unfolds. A partial-narrative deity is a distorted image.

Those who hold a similar theology to Driscoll's, for example, lift a single image of Jesus from the book of Revelation. This image draws on violent imagery, but reading it literally or in isolation from the full sweep of the Bible is deeply problematic. The overwhelming picture of Jesus presented in the New Testament Gospels and elsewhere is a loving Servant who rules by self-giving, not by force.

If you worship the full-narrative Jesus of the New Testament, you're worshipping a Jesus who was beaten up and executed. Hyping a tattooed Jesus may spark a rowdy crowd to cheer and whoop, but this image is difficult to reconcile with a crucified Jesus who remains silent when accused and never punches back. The Jesus of the Gospels seems almost unrecognizable when compared to the bloodthirsty God that so many Christians imagine.

A whole-narrative understanding of God sets our minds at ease, calms our nerves, and tattoos our hearts with the compassionate kindness of a deity who whips us up in a tornado of love and mercy. This view is not only truer, but it has powerful positive effects.

The Marymount Manhattan College study cited earlier demonstrates that talking about and believing in a benevolent God can lead to a significant reduction in anxiety, paranoia, obsession, compulsion, and other psychiatric symptoms. An additional study by the *Journal of Health Care Chaplaincy* concludes that "activating a patient's own beliefs that God is loving and caring, and/or that God positively intervenes in one's life, would be a particularly potent method of reducing anxiety" and other forms of psychosis.[11]

Before more conservative readers throw this book into the fire and roast hot dogs with the heat, I'm not suggesting that Christians tear out the Bible passages that speak of judgment or wrath or righteous anger. Rather, I'm suggesting we refuse to let partial images of God dominate our minds and deform our behavior and instead step back to see God in the context of the larger story.

God is not a tattooed punk who sends tornados to kill innocents and dangles sinners over a fire à la Jonathan Edwards. Comprehending God isn't easy, but we can at least say that God is an all-compassionate parent whose first name is Love. When you think of God in this way, don't be surprised if you become more like God and less like Mike Tyson.

14

Fall: Scientific Quandaries and the Beauty of You

Sometimes answers evade us because we've grown obsessed with the wrong questions. For me, this evasion dressed in a theological tracksuit and arrived without warning.

Whenever I want to immerse myself in the city, I grab a book, ride the subway three stops, and enter the chaos of Union Square Park. It's an odd place to read, with all the dogs barking, babies crying, squirrels pestering, and street performers performing. Still, I've come to enjoy the buzz and have learned to let it soothe me like white noise.

This particular day, I devoured a book on theology and genetics. I grew up in a faith tradition that was, at best, suspicious of science. As a biology and chemistry major at the conservative Liberty University, my "creation studies" classes argued against some of science's cornerstone claims about the origins of life.

As the years passed, I dug deeper and began to understand that believers didn't have to choose between faith and science. The two can coexist in harmony. The book I read in Union Square explained that one of the beliefs I had held since childhood was a genetic impossibility—that Adam and Eve, the first humans created by God and first to sin against God, could not have actually existed and was an allegorical story.

I left Union Square that day in a tailspin because the story of Adam and Eve had dramatic implications for my theology. Because of this story, I had accepted the claim that when this couple sinned by eating the fruit of a tree that God said was off-limits, all humans experienced the ominously labeled "the Fall." This was not just their story; it was all our stories. All humans have been touched by sin, the story said, and therefore we needed rescue. Christianity's rescue came in the form of Jesus. If Adam and Eve never existed, then maybe I didn't need Jesus as much as I thought.

Over the following weeks, this conundrum became a toppled domino triggering a cascade of vexing questions about faith and science, the origin of life, the existence of Adam and Eve, and most importantly, whether the Fall had happened or not.

When the voices in my head grew too contentious and too loud, I took all my scientific quandaries to my pastor. Perhaps he could help me choose faith over science and restore my confidence in the theological system I had been living with for more than two decades. When I asked him to prove to me that the Fall had happened, he turned my obsession on its head.

> The Fall is not just a long-ago event that we squint to see in our rearview mirrors but an ongoing reality we struggle to live with every day.

It's not that I was asking bad questions, he said, but perhaps I was missing the point. Maybe I was thinking about the word *fall* all wrong. I was cross-examining it through a pair of rational and scientific spectacles—the lens given to me by a tradition that had turned the strange, mysterious book of Genesis into a scientific textbook.

What if I unfurled my fingers and let go of those questions for a moment? What if I began to replace questions about the historicity of the story and instead welcomed questions about the truth of the story?

"Whether or not you agree that the Fall *happened*," he said, "we can all agree that the fall *happens*."

The story of the Fall is true, no matter what genetics claim, and reveals that:

- Humans often choose to cross boundaries that should not be crossed.
- Humans often partake of what is better left untouched.
- Humans resist notions of authority, desiring to seize control of our own destinies.
- Humans are prone to hiding our mistakes even when we know they are obvious to those closest to us.
- Humans' dumb choices, destructive habits, and deceptions have consequences—often separating us from the people and places we most love.
- Humans' shame is always met with God's grace.

The Fall, as many Christians believe, may have been a historical event involving a human couple thousands of years ago. I do not know. But I am certain that the notion of the Fall is one of the truest I've ever encountered.

The Fall is not just a long-ago event that we squint to see in our rearview mirrors but an ongoing reality we struggle to live with every day.

A striving that comes up short.

A moment when we realize yet again that we are naked and ashamed and in need of divine loincloths.

This is the point.

May we never miss it.

15

Sin: Pocket Nails and a Mountain of Metaphors

Bible scholar Scot McKnight had an unusual practice in a class he used to teach called "Jesus of Nazareth" at a Christian college. When each lecture concluded, he would ask his students to recite the Lord's Prayer together. He believed this was instructive because it sums up Jesus' ministry, but also because the prayer includes the phrase: "forgive us our sins." He thought his students needed to hear the word *sin* more often.

The practice was not popular among his students for two reasons. Some said they couldn't recall hearing about *sin* in any church service. Such a foreign word was jarring to these students. Others claimed to be offended at the word "because it was negative and harmful."[1] Many grew up in religious communities where the word was shouted and screamed and fashioned into a billy club to beat down and beat up. As a result, they never utter the word.

Sin has fallen on hard times these days.

In the South, where I was raised, the word *sin* was spoken often and loud. God was described as a pissed-off parent, and we were petulant children who couldn't help but mess up. *Sin* was the laundry list of our misdoings, always framed in terms of condemnation rather than confession. It was an authoritarian's attempt to scold others rather than choosing to disclose some embarrassing failing in his or her own life. The grammar invoked in such scoldings was second person *you* (and not first person *me* or plural *we*).

A friend of mine told me that when she was part of her church's youth group, her youth pastor handed each middle schooler a long nail. These young Christians were then encouraged to keep the nail in their pockets at all times. Whenever they committed a sin, they were told to reach into their pocket and press the nail into their palm. This would remind them of the pain God supposedly felt because of their sinful actions.

Some of those young people shrugged off the activity, but for others it fused painful feelings to the word *sin*. No wonder this word has been packed in mothballs and stuffed in the attic. But the larger problem is not our silence about sin but rather our fractured understandings of its meaning. The notion of sin, and its corresponding meaning, morphs throughout the Bible and Christian history. The dominant conception of this sacred term transformed over time. The history of *sin* is a case study for the way sacred terms, like all words, change.

The earliest notions of sin in Judaism drew on the metaphor of a stain. It is something that marked us and awaited cleansing. In this metaphor, the spit and polish of forgiveness was not sufficient to completely wipe away sin. The effects of the sin lingered, even tainting the sinners' offspring after they had died. The book of Exodus, for example, talks about sin staining a family tree for up to four generations.[2]

A different metaphor eventually dominated among early writers of the Jewish Bible: sin as a *weight*. Whenever a person or a people broke God's laws, sin was the weight that was lowered onto the people's shoulders. This mass would be dragged around until it was lifted—not by way of individual repentance, typically, but rather corporate ritual.

One of the starkest pictures of this occurs in the book of Leviticus with descriptions of the Day of Atonement. The high priest removed the sins of the people via a scapegoat. An animal would be brought to the temple, and the high priest would lay both of his hands on the goat's head, placing the weight of the people's sin on the goat. The scapegoat would then run into the wilderness, where it would vanish from the sight of the people as well as God. By some mystical mechanism, this lifted the weight of sin from the shoulders of the people.[3]

> The dominant notion of sin, and its corresponding meaning, morphs throughout the Bible and Christian history. It is a case study for the way sacred terms, like all words, change.

This way of understanding sin dominates the early writings of the Old Testament. But there is a rather large gap—perhaps half a millennia—between the early writings and the late writings of the Jewish Bible. During this period, the Hebrew language underwent a significant transformation as the dialect of the region changed and a new lingua franca, Aramaic, reshaped it. Perhaps unsurprisingly, the definition of sacred terms like *sin* morphed during this time too.[4]

The notion of sin as a weight was replaced by the idea that sin is like a *debt* that is owed to a lender.[5] By the time Jesus arrives on the scene in first-century Palestine, this understanding of sin had stolen the show and replaced earlier notions.[6] You will be hard pressed to find the sin-as-weight metaphor anywhere in the New Testament or other Jewish writings during this period.

Jesus speaks of sin predominantly in terms of a debt that needs to be paid off. We recite his famous prayer by saying, "Forgive us our sins," but a literal interpretation of Jesus' words is, "Forgive us our debts." And when he wants to describe what the kingdom of God is like, he talks about a servant who owes a colossal monetary debt to a king. Paul follows suit. In

Romans, he talks about "the wages of sin," an idea that would sound strange to earlier Jewish writers. But Paul doesn't seem to mind. He's speaking God in the world that *exists,* not the world that *existed* once.[7]

This new definition of *sin* allowed the biblical authors to add a feature to their understanding of the concept. If your sin is like making a debit out of some otherworldly account, then you can make deposits too. The New Testament, for example, speaks of "treasures in heaven" that are stored up by those who perform good deeds.[8]

Early Jesus followers carry this notion of sin forward as they develop Christian theology. In some regards, it served them well. Giving alms to the poor, for example, became a central tenet of the well-lived Christian life. But this framework also had its drawbacks. In the Middle Ages, Christian theologians attached price tags to certain sins. Soon the church was selling indulgences so people could settle their sin accounts. Faith itself was understood in transactional terms, something that was attained by good works or by giving money to the church, rather than divine grace.

In some ways, the Protestant Reformation was as much a linguistic revolution as a theological one. The notion of sin as a debt had metathesized into something that no longer worked. Martin Luther and other revolutionaries hit the Reset button on the vocabulary of faith. While Luther never wrote about sin specifically, the topic is mentioned in nearly all his writings.[9] And his writings started a rethinking of the dominant metaphor of sin as a debt.

The rethinking soon rippled out across Europe's burgeoning Protestantism. Following the Reformation, the Christian religion splintered into an assortment of denominations. And this schism shattered the Christian understanding of sin into a mountain of meanings and metaphors that continue until today.

Some talk about sin primarily as a "problem." It is an obstacle that we face, a puzzle that needs solving. Others speak of sin as a "sickness." It's an illness, a malady, a vexing condition. Still others speak of sin as "lawlessness." Sin is, put simply, breaking God's rules.[10]

Like all metaphors, these reveal a part of the truth but not the whole truth. When we speak of sin as a problem, it implies that God is the solution to what ails us. But this isn't the whole truth, because God doesn't just solve the problem of sin in the world without us. When we speak of sin as a sickness, it expresses the notion that sin infects all of us at some point during our lives and is often contagious. But this isn't the whole truth, because a sickness is something that happens to you and you are not responsible for its effects. Punishment for an evildoer would never be justified if sin as sickness told us everything about it. When we speak of sin as lawlessness, it helps us to understand the ways in which our everyday behaviors may be unloving and harmful, and it leaves us responsible for our actions. [11] But it doesn't tell the whole truth, because it can turn God into a strict disciplinarian with a list of dos and don'ts while subtly encouraging us humans to derive our worth from being on our best behavior.

We run off the tracks when we overemphasize one of the many ways of talking about sin to the exclusion of others. Which makes me wonder if there might be a way of describing the omnipresent force of destruction and devastation on earth that is roomy enough for all these metaphors and more.

A theologian friend of mine provides a definition that I find helpful. She says that life itself is the only framework comprehensive enough to explain sin. After all, sin affects all of life. Since Jesus described himself as the One who came to give abundant life to all creation, we might think of sin as anything that robs us of the fullness of life—or something we've done that robs others of the fullness of life. Sin as a thief, if you will.

Some people use the word *flourishing* to describe the abundant life, so they describe sin as anything that does not promote flourishing. And the Jewish scriptures use the word *shalom*—a state of total peace and harmony in life—to get at this idea. Shalom is, as some have said, "the way things are supposed to be." All things reconciled. We might say that sin is whatever contributes to life being less than what God intends. [12]

Under this definition, sin is a sickness, a problem, and a failure to live by ethical rules that promote life. It's like a stain, a weight, and in some way, a debt. It is brokenness and messiness and mistakes. Sin is a death dealer and a life stealer.

This definition frees us to affirm that God hates sin. Not because God is an angry rule-maker. But because God loves us without constraint. God wants each of us to live the abundant life. God wants peace for us. God wants shalom for us. God wants us to flourish. He wants us to recognize the divine imprint in others and support their flourishing. Any force that resists the abundant life is called "sin," and this is a force to which God stands opposed.

Sin is a reality faced by all—the cost of life on earth. It mars everything. Sin is present in workdays and weekends, in family lives, in public policy, and in private thoughts.

Even our good deeds often have sinful motivations. A friend of mine is a great philanthropist, but he gives money so that others will consider him charitable. Another friend attends every baseball game his son plays in, but he is driven by a need to be better than his own absentee father. The most selfless acts are often touched by sinful impulses.

We cannot understand what we will not name, and we cannot confront it unless we name it rightly. By acknowledging sin exists, we affirm our common condition, recognize that no one is better than another, and recommit to work for the flourishing of all. By speaking it out loud, we admit that life is not always as it should be. By confessing it, we remind ourselves that forgiveness is always available to bullies and so-called snowflakes and everyone in between.

Speaking such a word requires people—you and me—to admit that we are deeply flawed and often engage in destructive behavior. This first step may be the most formidable of them all.

16

Grace: Umbrellas
and Unmerited Favor

There are as many Christian definitions of the word *grace* floating around as there are Christians.

The *Catechism of the Catholic Church* says that grace is "favor, the free and undeserved help that God gives us to respond to his call to become children of God, adoptive sons, partakers of the Divine nature and of eternal life." Pentecostal Christians speak of a first grace as a gift of God extending forgiveness upon conversion, and a second grace as a divine gift that makes humans holy. Orthodox Christians might tell you "grace is the very life that flows naturally and eternally from God."[1] Calvinist Christians might say that grace is "God's disposition to elect for himself a people apart from any of their works."[2]

The range of meanings is wide; each definition contains its own flourishes and caveats. But when I began to research common understandings of *grace* among modern American Christians, it struck me that while popular definitions vary, they also share a common thread. Each definition of *grace* I encountered, without exception, contained at least three components:

1. Something that flows from God to humans, usually leading to "salvation"
2. Something that God offers freely—an undeserved gift
3. Something that God offers joyfully[3]

This list might be on track, but it is also incomplete. It only speaks of the grace *of* God. Or more precisely, the grace *from* God. Which is amazing and can transform how you think about God. But what about the other kind of grace? The kind that we humans offer to each other?

The idea that we are called to be people of grace, by some mechanism in which God's grace fills us up and spills out into the world, is both ancient and Christian. The Bible encourages us to infuse grace into our actions and even our words. If we are the offspring of a gracious God, it stands to reason that we are to be gracious children. Grace is woven into our DNA.

Unfortunately, modern American Christians haven't much to say about this kind of grace. Which is probably why when you ask nonreligious people what they think of Christians, they will often say "judgmental" or "hypocritical" before "gracious."

Twenty-first century Christians desperately need to develop a more robust understanding of this important word. But trespassers beware. Talking about *grace* may not be a comfortable conversation.

> Grace on the receiving end is a lovely flower.
> Grace on the giving end is the pits.

> Grace on the receiving end is free, no doubt.
> Grace on the giving end may cost you everything.

> Grace on the receiving end is joyful.
> Grace on the giving end is often painful.

Just a few months after relocating to Brooklyn, I encountered the second kind of grace. This marked the first time I remember despising the city. I was only five blocks from my apartment, en route to meet a friend for dinner, when thunder clapped and the sky fell. As a New York newbie, I wasn't yet in the habit of checking the weather each time I ventured outside my apartment building. I was unarmed and unprepared, in desperate need of an umbrella.

In the distance, I spotted a grocery store and dashed in its direction. Twenty-nine dollars seemed like hefty freight for an umbrella, but I was desperate. I paid the cashier and ventured back into the downpour.

I had walked only two blocks when I noticed her. An elderly woman walking in stride with me as the rain pelted her sideways. She had also apparently forgotten to check the weather before departing, and she was now soaking wet as a consequence. The fabric of her dress was bunched up and dripping, and her drenched silver hair fell like a dark curtain around her head. With each step I took, that good ole Christian guilt welled up inside of me.

By the time I reached her, a spring fired in my elbow and I handed her my new umbrella, the price tag still dangling. "Here you go, ma'am," I said. "Why don't you take this?" Without a word and avoiding eye contact, she snatched the handle as if entitled to it and lumbered off.

> The idea that we are called to be people of grace, by some mechanism in which God's grace fills us up and spills out into the world, is ancient and Christian.

I rolled my eyes—*How could she have been so rude?*—but I had no time to dwell on the encounter. I was back where I had started, wet and exposed. With haste, I jogged to a bodega on the approaching corner and purchased a second umbrella.

Another two blocks, another helpless person approaching. The man sat in a motorized wheelchair that appeared to need a tune-up. With one arm he steered, and with the other, he held a plastic shopping bag over his head to shield him from the storm. A few more steps, and I felt the nudge again. Upon reaching him, I handed him my second umbrella with a kind encouragement. He didn't even slow down, grabbing the umbrella like it was a baton and he was an Olympic relay runner. Not a word to me.

Ingrate!

By this point, I was seething and grumbling and miserable. My fabric shoes were squishing beneath me, and my feet were bone cold. I was late for dinner, and there wasn't another store to procure an umbrella between me and the restaurant. I broke into a sprint and raced toward my destination.

One block away—I could smell the restaurant already—I was forced to stop at the crosswalk. Water dribbled down my face onto my already soaked shirt. *Well, at least it can't get any worse,* I thought.

Just then, a speeding SUV bolted through the intersection and barreled through a muddy water puddle so large you'd need a boating license to cross it. Like in a movie, a wave of water waist-high slapped me and forced me to stumble backward. The light turned green, and I walked the final distance. Denim clung to my legs, now colder than cold.

I entered the restaurant brooding in silence. While my friend surveyed my rain-soaked disposition, I removed my shoes and hung my socks on the coat rack. He didn't say anything at first, and neither did I. But he finally broke the quiet and asked me what had happened.

"Grace happened, that's what," I replied. "And I hate it—and I love it."

17

Brokenness: Reparative Therapy and Our Aversion to Responsibility

I shot straight up in bed, sweat beading and out of breath. Halfway through my journey to speak God from scratch, all I could think about was the meaning of sacred terms. A word had surfaced from my past, begging for my repentance.

I'd used the word in a public forum four years earlier when a blogger questioned my sexual orientation and my life was thrown into disarray. At the time, I knew I needed to respond in some way, and my left-shoulder devil told me to flat-out lie. "Just say it isn't true, and it will all go away," he whispered, red tail whipping the air. Then my right-shoulder angel spoke sense: "If you kick the can down the road any longer, the price will be steep. Too steep."

I needed to speak honestly, but how?

The problem with telling the truth is that you don't always know what the truth is. A dozen friends stepped in to advise me, and their recommendations often conflicted with each other. I was under duress from bloggers online who seemed to have nothing better to do than speculate about the private lives of others—particularly those in Christian communities.

Perhaps of most importance, I was only now confronting questions that I had not given myself permission to consider in nearly thirty years of life.

Significant questions. I stared into the dark corridors of my soul, facing questions about my theology and my identity, my faith and my future. No small matters.

My friend let me answer a few questions on his blog to provide some clarity on the matter, and in that interview, I used a term to describe myself and my sexual orientation that plagued me many years later: *brokenness*.

Uttering these ten letters seemed harmless at the time, but now they haunted me. Confused in the moments between REM-state sleep and full-on alertness, I had just enough coherence to realize that I had misused that sacred word then, that I regretted the decision now, and that I would never use that term again in such a way.

> In a world where *sin* has become a dirty word, *brokenness* has become all the rage. We use it to describe circumstances we don't like, and often, to label people who don't fit our notions of the good Christian life.

In a world where *sin* has become a dirty word, *brokenness* has become all the rage among Christians. We use it to describe circumstances that we don't like, and often, to label people who don't fit our notions of the "good Christian life." I've heard Christians use the word *broken* to refer to divorced people, disabled people, depressed people, suicidal people, gay and lesbian people, transgender people. In these cases, the word has become a cudgel to malign and marginalize "other" individuals who are no more and no less in need of God's grace than the labelers themselves. The b-word has become a stepladder to describe people we don't understand or like or want to make space for.

The word seems fitting for some situations. If a happy marriage is a picture of wholeness, then *brokenness* seems appropriate to describe a cheating husband leaving his wife and children to fend for themselves. If a healthy life is a picture of wholeness, then a diagnosis of terminal pancreatic cancer likely fits the description. But what about sexual orientation?

In a world where gay marriage is a divisive issue in the American church, it's no wonder that people of faith discuss it clumsily. In such a moment, many believers who are uncomfortable with any expression of marriage or family that falls outside traditional bounds talk about LGBT people as broken. Four years earlier, I used the word this way to describe myself. But now I wondered whether *broken* was really the best word.

Calling something or someone *broken* implies that the person or thing can be fixed. While sexuality may be more fluid than some progressives admit, it is also far more difficult to manipulate than many conservatives wish. Whatever one believes about the morality of same-sex relationships, we can agree that sexual orientation is not like a light switch that can be flipped on or off by a well-trained hand—even a hand that holds a Bible. Sexuality is a mysterious part of who we are as humans, like it or not. If you run from it in an effort to escape it—as many of my friends have—you'll end up back where you started, except more frustrated and defeated.

We are not the first people, or even the first Christians, to use this term to label LGBT people and homosexual orientation this way. In his book *Psychoanalysis and Male Homosexuality*, Kenneth Lewes says that speaking about sexual orientation as "brokenness" might be traced back as far as the nineteenth century when some began to see homosexuality as a mental health disorder.

By the start of the American cultural revolution in the 1960s, many mental-health professionals and politicians supported the idea that homosexuality was a DSM-classified disorder that could be cured through therapy. Clergy and believers would recommend prayer and healing services in addition to psychological "treatment."

Attempts to change sexual orientation were not for the faint of heart. They included genital electroshock therapy, masturbatory reconditioning, and giving patients nausea-inducing drugs while forcing them to view homosexual erotica.

They seem shocking now, but these practices were quite mainstream until the last half century.

"One reason why homosexuals are so rarely cured is that they rarely try treatment," proclaimed a 1965 *Time* magazine article. "Too many of them actually believe that they are happy and satisfied the way they are."[1]

As mental health practitioners began to honestly observe the results of these misguided therapies, they found them to be woefully ineffective and often damaging. Sexual orientation was far more resistant to coercion than some believed. In 1974, the American Psychiatric Association voted to remove homosexuality from its list of mental health disorders. This inflamed many conservatives, especially the Christians among them, who responded by launching a handful of well-funded ex-gay ministries.

But these efforts could not outrun reality. Scientific studies continued to provide evidence of the harm caused by efforts to "fix" this "brokenness." The author of the main study cited in support of ex-gay therapy apologized and admitted that his data was tainted, unreliable, and had been misinterpreted. Every major medical and health-care group with a stake in the game systematically repudiated the practice as harmful. Many high-profile ex-gay leaders eventually defected to the other side or were exposed as frauds.[2]

While ex-gay therapy is now largely spurned, even by many conservative Christians, the ideology remains in our use of the word *broken* to refer to sexual minorities.

The concept of brokenness is rarely mentioned in the Bible. The closest example might be when the psalmist writes about a broken heart and a crushed spirit.[3] The writer references something that happens to us, rather than something we are. And instead of speaking about brokenness as making someone less than, the author says that God is especially close to those in such a state. Talk about a paradigm shifter.

That night when I was woken from my sleep, drenched in sweat and regret, I knew that the word *broken* is itself broken and in need of repair. Sure, the word still has some life left in it. We should speak freely about "broken marriages" and "broken political systems" and "broken hearts." We use these not as tools of marginalization but as signposts of hope reminding us that mending is possible.

But perhaps the time has come to stop using *brokenness* in ways that do not make sense and cause harm to others. My grandpa used to say that if something ain't broken, then you shouldn't try to fix it. I say that if something can't be fixed, then it probably ain't broken.

18

Blessed: Hollow Hashtags and Marble Toilets

Have you ever met someone so genuine and precious his or her mere presence serves as an apologetic that God really exists? For me, one of those people is Kate Bowler.

We met on a writing retreat. Kate is an expert on the history of the prosperity gospel, a belief system that asserts that God offers health and wealth to obedient believers. After cross-examining the prosperity gospel in light of her current situation, she discovered that one word sat at the core of this Christian framework: *blessed.* The word was "shorthand for the prosperity message" and described a state in which a believer received God's favor—usually in the form of physical healing, increased wealth, or personal happiness.[1]

This theology is heavily promoted by flashy televangelists and megachurch pastors who are paid handsomely and boast large properties or holdings. Because they believe material possessions are a sign of God's goodness, opulence isn't a source of shame, but of pride.

In 2007, for example, the United States Congress decided to investigate six ministries that promote this type of thinking. What they uncovered was a level of lavishness that might surprise some of the donors who have scraped pennies in order to support these preachers.

Missouri pastor Joyce Meyer was asked to explain the nature of a litany of purchases that were made by her tax-exempt ministry—not the least of which being a $23,000 "commode with a marble top."[2] Texas televangelists Kenneth and Gloria Copeland reside in a $6.3 million lakeside "parsonage."[3]

When it was reported that Kenneth Copeland used ministry money to purchase a private jet worth millions, he argued that he simply could not ride on commercial planes because they were full of "a bunch of demons" and that seat belt restrictions wouldn't let him drop to his knees for prayer at will.[4]

Copeland isn't the only televangelist flying in luxury. Creflo Dollar made a plea to all his Christian donors to fund an "airplane project," which was shorthand for "pay $65 million to purchase a Gulfstream G650 luxury jet." Dollar already owned a private plane, but according to his ministry's website, the new jet would allow Dollar to "safely and swiftly share the Good News of the Gospel worldwide."

Dollar defended the decision, and his congregation responded with cheers and a standing ovation. "You cannot stop and you cannot curse what God has *blessed*," Dollar said.[5]

Those of us who find ourselves outside the prosperity gospel movement may be quick to judge their use of the word, but perhaps we should self-reflect instead. Though Bowler credits the prosperity gospel movement with popularizing the word *blessed*, she says that over the last decade "'being blessed' has become a full-fledged American phenomenon."[6]

If you're not convinced, just hop on social media and search #blessed. You'll discover the hashtag applied to photos of Caribbean vacations, engagement rings, luxury vehicles wrapped in oversized Christmas bows. As *New York Times* writer Jessica Bennett jokes, "God has, in fact, recently *blessed* my network with dazzling job promotions, coveted speaking gigs, the most wonderful fiancés ever, front row seats at Fashion Week, and nominations for many a '30 under 30' list."[7]

Rolex-wearing prosperity preachers are easy targets, of course, but many ordinary Christians speak of blessings in similar, if subtler, ways. We commandeer the word to humble-brag about our health, wealth, and good fortune.

In some ways, how Americans often use the term *blessing* isn't far from the way some ancient Jews did. The word for "blessing" in Hebrew, *barak*, originally meant to kneel, or literally "to bend the knee." A blessing was usually passed from a person of higher standing to a person of lower standing, and the blessed person would kneel to receive it. The word was as prominent among the ancient Jews as it is today, appearing more than six hundred times in the Old Testament. A blessing was a sign of special favor and included everything from a spouse to pregnancy, affluence to a general sense of joy.

One glaring difference is that the ancient Jewish understanding of this word is rooted in humility. Today, it is often tethered to pride. We don't just receive blessings with bended knee; we declare them to the world. This not only potentially stirs up the worst parts of ourselves, but it also can inflict pain on those who don't experience the same kinds of blessings we do. Trends like #blessed are amplified in our social media–driven culture—those without the blessing are forced to witness those who've received.

After spending a decade studying the prosperity gospel, Bowler received horrific news: she had stage IV colon cancer. As a young mother, she struggled to understand how the prosperity gospel's understanding of God, illness, and blessings made sense of her condition. Dying from cancer and leaving behind a husband and child doesn't look like God's favor.[8]

Bowler realized that modern conceptions of the word *blessed* are problematic, in part, because it "blurs the distinction between two very different categories: gift and reward. It can be a term of pure gratitude. 'Thank you, God. I could not have secured this for myself.' But it can also imply that it was deserved. 'Thank you, me. For being the kind of person who gets it right.'"[9]

By the time the New Testament is composed, the dominant ancient Jewish meaning of *blessing* has been replaced by a new conception. The word becomes less materialistic and more spiritual, less external and more internal. A blessing is still a sign of God's special favor, but it refers now to kindness, forgiveness, and peace. When Jesus preaches his Sermon on the Mount, the term undergoes a radical evolution. Jesus calls "blessed" those who are pure in heart and poor in spirit, the meek and mournful, those who are peacemakers and persecuted.

What if we began thinking about blessings as immaterial and internal, spiritual and supernatural? It's difficult to imagine attaching #blessed to these sorts of virtues today and having the post go viral. But I bet we'd be better for it.

But there is yet another deeper, richer way to understand this sacred term. When Greek speakers adopt the word for "bless" from Hebrew speakers, the definition morphs from "to kneel" to "to praise." A blessing is not just something we receive, but it is something we should offer to others, even to God. And the purpose of receiving blessings is to bless others.

What if we stopped hashtagging blessings and started handing them out instead? Maybe that is what prosperity in this world truly looks like. Perhaps that is what it means to be #blessed.

19

Neighbor: Mister Rogers and the Global Refugee Crisis

When ISIS militants in Syria beheaded American war correspondent James Foley, I was only a few miles from the country's border, interviewing refugees in a Lebanese tent settlement. The news that ISIS forces were targeting journalists in the region struck me like an anvil, but I did not leave. I could not leave. The Syrian refugee children's stories deserved to be told.

Thirteen-year-old Mohamed, for example, recounted a story of playing outside when a rebel sniper's bullet penetrated his cousin's skull. Instant death. When his uncle rushed to the body, a sniper shot him in the face, killing him too. A Syrian military tank later ran over both corpses. Mohamed was forced to watch his family members' bodies rot from a distance.

Mohamed's classmates told me similar stories. They spoke of bombing, corpses, torture, people who lost limbs. Almost all showed signs of psychological trauma and social dysfunction, including speech impediments and panic attacks. They either shrank back when you tried to touch them or clung to you for affection.

Three-year-old Suheib hadn't spoken a word since arriving at a shelter in Taanayel, Lebanon. Every time a plane flew overhead, he ran in terrified circles. His seven-year-old brother, Hamza, suffered from night terrors.

Their mother told me that Hamza's response to the violence he witnessed in Syria confounded her: "He would laugh and cry at the same time while shivering."[1]

I recorded similar stories for nearly two weeks before returning home, where Americans were debating whether to allow Syrian refugees into our country. Arriving back to my apartment, I phoned a friend—a Christian of the southern conservative variety—to process the horrors I'd witnessed. He listened patiently to my stories and then responded, "That's sad, but we can't be responsible for those children. We've got our hands full here in America with our own problems."

This kind of "America First" thinking would not fully metastasize in American public life until the political ascension of Donald Trump two years later. But the narrow worldview confounded me even then.

"But what if those children *were* your neighbors?" I asked him.

"In that case, I guess I would have to do something to help them," he said.

———

I recalled this conversation after launching my journey to speak God from scratch, and it convinced me to explore the word *neighbor*. If we are supposed to love those whom the word describes, we ought to pause and ponder what the word means to us and who qualifies.

The English word *neighbor* derives from the words *nigh* or "near" and *gebur* or "dweller." In the literal sense of the English word, a neighbor is someone who lives near you. If we are to love our neighbors, as Jesus instructed, as the second greatest commandment, we must care for those who live in close proximity to us. But in a world of hustle, bustle, and business, this simple task can seem formidable.

Before I moved to New York City, I resided in the suburbs of Atlanta. When I returned home from work or errands each day, I raised my garage door with the push of a button and closed it just as quickly. Nestled in my domestic cocoon, I kept to myself with ease.

I tried reaching out one Labor Day. A group of young people from my church came to my house. They assembled chocolate chip cookies and banana bread on platters. Marching around the neighborhood in pairs, we attempted to offer these sweet treats to each house. About a third of my neighbors peered through their blinds but would not open their doors. Some declined the gift by shouting through a closed door. A few were friendly and grateful, but at the end of the day, more than half of the platters remained. In the five years I lived in that house, I learned the names of only two of my neighbors.

> In many American communities, it's easy to avoid knowing or being known by one's neighbors. We have forgotten how to love and prioritize the people who live alongside us.

In many American communities, it's easy to avoid knowing or being known by one's neighbors. As a result, we have forgotten how to love and prioritize the people who live alongside us.

Jesus' understanding of *neighbor,* however, includes but also stretches beyond the fence posts of the English definition. In one of the Bible's most famous passages, a legal expert asks Jesus, "Who is my neighbor?" The Rabbi replies by spinning a story about a man who got the crap beat out of him by bandits and was left to die on the roadside. Two men passed the man by and refused to help. A third man, a despised Samaritan, stopped to care for the injured victim.

"Which of these three do you think was a neighbor to the man who fell into the hands of robbers?" Jesus asked.

"The one who had mercy on him," the legal expert replied.

Jesus instructed him, "Go and do likewise."[2]

The Samaritan in Jesus' story didn't dwell near the victim. Samaritans lived and worshipped in a segregated community, so he almost certainly didn't reside in close proximity to the bedraggled man. He just happened to be on the same road that day. So Jesus' definition of *neighbor* seems to be "anyone who is in need." They can live across the street or ten thousand miles away in a refugee camp.

This isn't the way many think of *neighbor* when they speak it today. In recent years, an isolationist ideal has been rising, narrowing the application of *neighbor* only to someone you can put eyes on personally. But Jesus' definition is similar to my earliest notions of this word, which were shaped by a thin, soft-spoken man named Fred—known to the world as Mister Rogers.

Childhood memories stick in my mind. I can hear the sound of the trolley bell, and visions of King Friday or Daniel Striped Tiger bring a smile to my face. I can see Mister Rogers slipping off his jacket and putting on one his cardigans, famously knitted by his mother, Carolyn. He said he was my friend, and I believed him.

During my formative years, Mister Rogers and I met often to talk about life, and his gentle candor made him the best neighbor any kid could ask for.

Rogers got into television because he "hated" the medium. During his senior year in seminary, he encountered television for the first time, and what he witnessed repulsed him. "I got into television," he once recounted, "because I saw people throwing pies at each other's faces, and that to me was such demeaning behavior. And if there's anything that bothers me, it's one person demeaning another. That really makes me mad!"[3]

In the wake of World War II, when men (many of them veterans), were having trouble expressing their feelings, Fred Rogers recognized that the children of these quiet giants might also have difficulty expressing their emotions. He worried that the type of programming that was becoming normative would spawn a generation of emotionally bankrupt Americans.

Faced with the decision to either sour on television itself or work to better the medium, he chose the latter and began pursuing a career in broadcasting. Fourteen years later, he created one of the most beloved American television shows of all time.

Each day he stood before a camera and spoke words that, like torches, illuminated his young viewers' minds and shaped entire generations of American children.

Fred Rogers knew the power his words contained, which is why he reviewed his shows and scripts with Dr. Margaret McFarland, a professor in the department of psychiatry at the University of Pittsburgh. Before taping an episode, a team of child psychology experts reviewed the script's effects on children's cognitive and emotional development.

He talked to children like adults, teaching kids to face the world's hard realities and not shrink back. Emotions should be embraced, not buried.

"The world is not always a kind place," he once said. "That's something all children learn for themselves, whether we want them to or not, but it's something they really need our help to understand."[4]

At seven or eight years old, I remember sitting cross-legged two feet from our boxy television. Mister Rogers didn't just talk to me; I often spoke back. I later learned many children responded in this way. Because the dialogue often felt so personal, it would sometimes trigger a verbal response from young viewers, a "byplay," in which they "may respond vocally to a question and Rogers, anticipating the reply, may follow through to his next point."[5] He imagined himself as something of a surrogate parent, which is why other children never appeared on the show. He didn't want to create a sentiment of sibling rivalry.

When Rogers encountered a child who watched faithfully, he might say, "Why, I think you've grown!" And the child often proudly responded, "I thought you'd notice that, Mister Rogers." Such responses proved that he had been successful in providing what he called "a neighborhood expression of care for children." That was the animating force behind his show and behind the message presented in each episode.

Rogers's approach to his craft and calling was the result of his Christian faith. Rogers was an ordained minister, and since he left seminary to pursue television, the local branch of his denomination gave him a special commission as an evangelist to children.

This unlikely TV evangelist seemed to be always aware that his vocational calling was originated from on high. He believed "the space between the television set and the viewer is holy ground," though he trusted God to do the heavy lifting. The wall of his office featured a framed picture of the Greek word for "grace," a constant reminder of his belief that he could use television "for the broadcasting of grace through the land." And before entering that office each day, Rogers would pray, "Dear God, let some word that is heard be yours."[6]

In 1998, *Esquire* reported the story of a young viewer of *Mister Rogers' Neighborhood* with an acute case of autism. The child had never spoken a word until one day he uttered, "X the Owl," the name of one of Mister Rogers's most popular puppets. And the boy had never looked his father in the eye either, until the day his dad said, "Let's go to the Neighborhood of Make-Believe." After this, the boy began speaking and reading, which inspired the father to visit Fred Rogers personally to thank him for changing his son's life.

Later in Rogers's life, he recounted the story of a child who was being abused by his biological parents, who reportedly "wouldn't even give him a winter blanket and wouldn't give him a bed to sleep in." Through encountering *Mister Rogers' Neighborhood*, the child began to hope that there were kind people in the world and became convinced that he too should be treated with respect. The child called an abuse hotline and was rescued. Even more stunning, the hotline operator who answered the phone adopted the boy.[7]

No matter which topic an episode featured, there was one word Rogers always spoke: *neighbor*. For him, a neighbor was not just the person who lived next door to you that you waved to when retrieving your mail. It may not be someone who looked like you or dressed like you or frequented the same coffee shop. It was anyone whose path you crossed, especially if that person was in need. Which is to say, Mister Rogers's definition was almost identical to Jesus'.

In 1999, when Fred Rogers was inducted into the Academy of Television Arts and Sciences Hall of Fame, he reflected on his career:

> *Fame* is a four-letter word. And like *tape* or *zoom* or *face* or *pain* or *life* or *love*, what ultimately matters is what we do with it. I feel that those of us in television are chosen to be servants. It doesn't matter what our particular job [is]. We are chosen to help meet the deeper needs of those who watch and listen, day and night. . . . Life isn't cheap. It's the greatest mystery of any millennium, and television needs to do all it can to broadcast that—to show and tell what the good in life is all about. But how do we make goodness attractive? By doing all we can to bring courage to those whose lives move near our own. By treating our "neighbor" at least as well as we treat ourselves and that to inform everything that we produce.[8]

Fred Rogers's entire existence seemed wrapped up with that legal expert's question to Jesus: "Who is my neighbor?" He did all he could to care for his neighbors—children of every color and creed, living across America and around the world—and he loved them well.

"You've made this day a special day by just your being you," he'd famously sign off. "There is no person in the whole world like you, and I like you just the way you are."

Rogers was right. There is no person in this world like you.

You have been created and called to love those in need, whether nestled in the suburban cocoon across the street or languishing in a refugee camp a million miles away.

As neighbors, we are bound to each other by humanity, not just proximity. Some in our culture believe we become stronger by being more inward-focused. That building walls and closing borders is better than the biblical mandate to invite all to the table. When it comes to neighborliness, we are connected by need, not nearness. If we began to understand *neighbor* in this way, it would be a beautiful day in our global neighborhood.

20

Pride: The Self-Esteem Movement and Tiptoe Terms

Light—no matter how essential or life giving—both illuminates and creates shadows. While Mister Rogers was a shining beacon who lit the way forward for generations of Americans by reminding them that they were special and worthy, the movement he sparked had a shadow side too.

Rogers's views came at a lynchpin moment in the history of Western psychology. Prior to this moment, common knowledge held that while humans had potential for much good, they were innately bad. Think of a beautiful apple with a rotten core. While we could affirm the beauty and deliciousness of the fruit itself, psychology was careful to point out that the fruit was foul from the seed.

This view was upended by psychologists in the middle of last century—when Rogers rose to prominence—who argued that humans are fundamentally good, even though they often have blemishes. Picture a tasty, shiny Honeycrisp apple with a couple skin-deep brown spots. This view asserted that environments of positive self-regard were necessary for raising healthy children.

This idea not only took root; it eventually took over. Teachers were being trained on how to boost their students' self-esteem and avoid mention of any potential flaws that might cause children to think less of themselves. Social scientists grew obsessed with studying the positive effects of positive self-images. Judges issued sentences of self-esteem rehabilitation for all manner of criminals, from swindlers to sex workers.

By the late twentieth century, the newly minted self-esteem movement dominated American life. Author Will Storr recounts:

> Heads big and small were systematically stuffed full of their own wondrousness. As the 1980s became the 1990s, schools and kindergartens began boosting self-esteem in classes, encouraging children to write letters to themselves, telling themselves how special they are. Five-year-olds in a Texas nursery were made to wear T-shirts that said 'I'm loveable and capable' and to recite the mantra daily. High school awards were dropped by the thousands, and grades were inflated to protect the esteem of low achievers.[1]

The result of this movement was, at least somewhat, beneficial. In the 1950s, only about 10 percent of fourteen- to sixteen-year-olds agreed with the statement "I am an important person." By the late 80s, this figure had risen to 80 percent.[2]

A measure of self-esteem is healthy for anyone. No one wants a society comprised of beat-down children who imagine themselves to be worthless subhumans. However, the self-esteem movement went much farther than embracing gifts, talents, and positive traits. The cultural addiction to self-esteem valued a praise-only approach to parenting above other methods.

Another effect of the self-esteem movement was a 180-degree redefinition of *pride*. The word was previously understood to be a negative word, referring to the obsession with self that lies at the heart of much evil. Christians, fueled by the Bible and by Dante, long believed pride to be a deadly sin. Those in a religious community who thought too highly of themselves were often admonished and brought down a peg.

In a whipcrack, this sacred term traded its rags for richer attire. Rather than warning that pride was self-congratulatory, arrogant, and an avoidable attribute, children were suddenly taught to "take pride in yourself and your work." The word didn't just take on a new meaning; it was exchanged for a photonegative of the original.

Recently, however, a new generation of psychologists with enough guts to challenge these sacrosanct notions of pride are discovering that our obsession with self-esteem has unwittingly spawned a whole slew of negative traits. Some children grew up to be self-obsessed narcissists who immerse themselves in a world of social media, which functions as a house full of mirrors. Others turned into fragile, overly sensitive creatures, unable to receive even the slightest criticism. But worst of all, many became bullies. So this evolution in esteem has turned dangerous.

In 1996, after reviewing the relevant scientific literature, social scientist Roy Baumeister concluded that the root cause of aggression and even violence was often "threatened egotism."[3] This is as true for the world's great dictators as it is for the measliest schoolyard bulldogs.

> To speak of pride in its fullness, we must recognize the light of authentic self-respect as well as the shadow of hubris.

"Dangerous people, from playground bullies to warmongering dictators," Baumeister said, "consist mostly of those who have highly favorable views of themselves."[4]

This brings us back to where we began—the light and its shadows.

Jessica Tracy, a psychology professor at the University of British Columbia and author of *Take Pride: Why the Deadly Sin Holds the Secret to Human Success*, helps us hold pride's glowing orb and expansive silhouette in balance. Her research reveals that this sacred term is not one thing, but two: authentic pride, which is an effective driver of human potential. And hubristic pride, which creates all kinds of problems.[5]

Authentic pride can be a powerful propellant, protecting against self-loathing and launching people to soaring heights in their professional lives. In this way, a certain kind of pride allows us to think of ourselves as God does: as "very good"[6] and beloved creations that possess inherent dignity and reflect the image of the Divine. If God thinks we have worth, then thinking of ourselves in similar fashion cannot be evil.

But pride's light also casts a shadow—hubris—that is cancerous and consuming, leading us to arrogance and aggrandizement. It does not just affirm one's worth, but it views one's worth as being greater than others'. Both the ancient Scriptures and modern psychology teach us this kind of pride is as deadly as arsenic.

To speak of pride in its fullness, we must recognize the light of authentic self-respect as well as the shadow of hubris. We must encourage each other to take pride in our work and selves, while guarding against the hubris that leads us to forget our relative smallness in the ever-expanding universe.

We do not need to spurn either Fred Rogers or Dante. We can recognize that both of them were getting at something worthy of attention. To love our neighbors as ourselves means to see that we are worth loving and those around us are too. This nuanced understanding of the word *pride* allows us to smile when we look into the mirror without feeling shame, knowing that God does the same when God sees us. But it also reminds us that behind that mirror-gazing face is a shadow that we ignore at our peril.

21

Saint: Protestant Holes and Holy Fools

Growing up Protestant in the American South, the only thing I learned about saints was that one day they were going to "come marching in" and I apparently wanted "to be in that number."

As a child, I once thumbed through a lost-and-found Bible that added the title *saint* to Matthew, Mark, Luke, and John. I remember a Sunday School teacher (oh-so-subtly) commenting that saints were just a way Catholics engaged in idol worship. But that was pretty much it. Decades later, I still didn't know what the heck the word *saint* meant.

My friend Matt unmasked my lack of knowledge about this word just after I moved to New York, when he asked me about my favorite saint. As a lapsed Roman Catholic from Boston, saints provided comfort to him. He had been impacted by his priests' Bible-based tales about stone tables, burning bushes, and flaming chariots, but the stories of saints felt more accessible and real. They told of ordinary, flawed people just like him.

As a person who studies religion for a living, I felt embarrassed when Matt asked me which saint was my favorite, and I didn't have an answer. I joked that I admired both Saint Laurent and the isle of Saint Martin, but I couldn't afford either one. After I walked away, Matt's question sent me on an expedition to play with this significant sacred term.

After poking around, I realized that many Protestant Christians are like me. They don't think much about saints. They don't celebrate feasts named after saints or retell their stories on special days. Some denominations are faithful in recognizing All Saints Day, but most don't even have a process for canonizing saints.

I now wonder if the Protestant tradition has a gaping saint-shaped hole in it. After digging into the stories of these mysterious men and women that some call saints, I concluded that it is a word and concept that can benefit all Christians. Indeed, we Protestants could use a few saints of our own.

Christians throughout history have interacted with saints in various ways. Eastern Orthodox believers gaze at them through icons and pass down their stories via hagiographies. Some Roman Catholics pray to them and ask for their help interceding with God. While such practices might make a good Protestant squirm, we can all benefit from viewing saints the way author Jacques Douillet does, as "those who march in front and give the example."

Conduct even a cursory review of the saints and you'll stumble over scores of misfits and outcasts. They were not considered balanced or stable or completely sane by all in their respective communities. Instead, this throng of oddballs was bold and countercultural and unashamed.

Saints embody what it means to follow Jesus when we are tempted to play it safe or go with the flow or opt for acceptability over conviction and commitment and passion.

Saints are, in the words of one writer, "eccentric, lopsidedly love-drunk people."[1] To wit:

Saint Christiana ministered to peasants in the medieval era, who were known for poor hygiene. Unfortunately, the smell of unpleasant body odors made her nauseous, and she'd often have to rush outside for fresh air to avoid vomiting.

Saint Philip Neri was an evangelist who loved to share the gospel. At Pentecost in 1544, he saw what appeared to be a globe of fire enter his mouth that caused his heart to dialate. For the rest of his life, spiritual emotion caused him great heart palpitations. Neri was a person of great joy and humor and has been called "God's clown."

Saint Basil, born in 330, used all his personal wealth to aid the poor and became a monk. He sometimes enraged the religious aristocracy by throwing stones at the homes of the rich for ignoring the poor. He was called *yurodivi* or "holy fool," though he was actually a great orator and accomplished statesman.

> **Modern-day Protestants often lionize those who've lived purpose-driven existences or have laid hold of their best life now. How unlike the saints of old.**

Saint Francis was on his way to join the crusades as a knight when God told him in a dream to turn around and go home. Francis then chose to live a life of poverty by giving away all his possessions, walking barefoot, and renouncing his father's inheritance. He would often pray and fast for days, without taking care of himself, causing people to question his sanity. He was known throughout Italy as Pazzo...or "madman."[2]

Modern-day Protestants often lionize those who've lived purpose-driven existences or have laid hold of their best life now. Winning for many modern Christians looks much more like the world's definition of material success than an early church understanding. How unlike the saints of old. How divergent from those nonconformists who dreamed dreams and saw visions and claimed to have heard Christ whisper in their ears.

The apostle Paul once said, "Our dedication to Christ makes us look like fools."[3] Spoken like a true saint.

Saints are people whose stories speak to us from above and ahead of us and whisper, "It's okay that you're a little crazy." They are reminders that if you follow Jesus, in the words of Flannery O'Connor, "You will know the truth and the truth will make you strange." I can't think of a God-speaker who wouldn't benefit from a few of those kinds of reminders.

22

Confession: Internet Vulnerability and Grace the Doorman

New places are less jarring and unkind with beloved friends nearby. That's why I was so glad when one of my closest confidants relocated from Orlando to New York City. Roxy has always been stylish and collected, the epitome of cool. Yet she is also a trusted friend with a penchant for loyalty and a gift for truth telling. She and I spent countless snow-blanketed hours in her tiny East Village apartment sipping mulled wine, talking about nothing and everything.

Roxy moved to New York City to rebuild her life after her decade-long marriage ended, so we sometimes discussed the situation and the healing process. In the middle of one emotional conversation, I suggested she blog about her divorce online. Perhaps writing would be therapeutic.

Roxy declined. As the former editorial director of *Relevant* magazine, a publication popular among young Christians, she was aware of the popularity of oversharing online. She'd been inundated with story pitches from people who were willing to auction off the messiest details of their personal lives just to see their names in print.

"There is power in sharing one's life online, but there is even more power in sharing it with those you love," she told me. "It's possible to be authentic online and inauthentic in your real life."[1]

Roxy had seen professionally, and personally, how sharing all the pain of one's journey could be problematic. Perhaps sharing would have benefitted some people, she admitted, and plenty of others had done that. But walking through it with a few friends and family members was difficult enough for her.[2]

"Sure, but Christians have always valued 'confession' haven't they?" I countered.

I squirmed almost as soon as I spoke it. I knew in my gut that the best meaning of that word might not fit this context. And just like that, I had a new word to explore.

In the internet and insta-celebrity age, where people often share too much with too many, *confession* is a misused sacred term often spoken in hopes of transforming personal pain into notoriety. Vulnerability and authenticity have become some of our society's highest values. When we speak or write, we do not only want to appear intelligent or helpful, we want to appear raw, honest, emotional, free of boundaries. When others bare their souls, we celebrate them for their bravery and courage.

Want to share the nasty details of your breakup? Fantastic.

Daddy issues? Go for it.

A play-by-play of your adult sibling rivalry? Sure.

Sexual struggles with your spouse? Why not?

Technological advances have not helped the situation. Today, blogs are ubiquitous on the internet (more than 200 million by some estimates), and social media networks continue to multiply. On these sites, people offer the most sensitive details of their lives. We publish, Facebook, pin, photograph, Tweet, snap, and squeeze our most intimate anecdotes into bite-sized offerings. (No wonder *overshare* was recently voted the word of the year.) [3]

Christians have a word to describe the act of being vulnerable with others: *confession*. The Latin root of this word is a combination of *com,* or "together" and *fateri,* or "to admit." This is the act of coming together with God or others and admitting all the failings that we've committed. The Christian Scriptures encourage us to practice this regularly.

In the internet and insta-celebrity age, where people often share too much with too many, *confession* is a misused sacred term often spoken in hopes of transforming personal pain into notoriety.

Given the emphasis on confessing in our faith tradition, it's unsurprising that we've adopted vulnerability as a Christian virtue. If you look at popular books by religious authors or blogs by spiritual leaders, you'll find ample evidence of this trend. Some seem to do this with the expectation of becoming *famous-ish*. Others operate from the hope of helping others who face similar struggles. Regardless, those who are willing to tear down the barriers to their personal lives are seen as noble and authentic.

Christianity has a long history of confessing. If you're Catholic, the process is formal. You step into a wooden box, then divulge all your sins to a priest sitting on the other side of a divider. The priest, acting as a representative for Jesus, forgives your sin and then assigns you a penance—a list of prayers you need to pray. The rest is up to you.

The process is a little less defined for Protestants. It begins, rather than concludes, with prayer. You tell God all your sins, which is interesting, since most Protestants believe God already knows everything you've done. But this is enough to qualify as confession, even though you may be encouraged or feel prompted to also divulge the details to a parent, friend, or accountability partner.

If you've ever made a confession to another person, you know how liberating it feels. The secret that lurked in the shadows is now called out into the sunlight. Your worries that someone may find out are eradicated, and you can rest easy without feeling like a fraud. But if confession is done poorly or to the wrong person, it can be damaging.

You have probably never heard the name Justin Hall, but as the world's first personal blogger, he started a trend that changed the world. While a student at Swarthmore College in Pennsylvania in 1994, he built a website and began keeping an online journal of his life. Without restraint, Hall aired his dirty laundry—all of it—handed over to any strangers with a computer and an internet connection.

Though the experience made Hall somewhat famous, it did not bring fulfillment. He sobbed regretfully about his behavior in a 2005 short film, *Dark Night*, took a ten-year internet hiatus, and now says he has learned to be "much more measured and mature in what I share online."[4]

Hall's cautionary tale is one many, including Christians, have failed to heed. Katelyn Beaty, an editor-at-large for *Christianity Today*, says we often witness Christian bloggers and leaders "confessing sins and shortcomings and dark pasts in inappropriate times and foolhardy ways. When vulnerability is unfettered by boundaries, it can become another way to earn spiritual points. It can feel like a performance of humility, as self-aware [as] a peacock surveying its own tail."[5]

When it comes to confession, your motivation matters. If you're seeking attention or adoration of your peers or clicks to your blog, this kind of confession isn't confession at all. It's voyeurism and performance.

In this regard, the internet is often a liability rather than an asset when it comes to confession. Psychology professor Gwendolyn Seidman noted, "Research examining interactions between people who have just met has shown that self-disclosure is often greater online than face-to-face."[6] Something about being online causes us to share things we might not otherwise divulge because of the validation we receive from our many faceless followers.

More importantly, the audience matters. Brené Brown writes in *Daring Greatly*, "Vulnerability is about sharing our feelings and our experiences with people *who have earned the right to hear them*."[7]

The Christian Scriptures encourage us to confess our struggles and sins to a God who loves us and is infinitely forgiving.[8] They also urge us to bare our souls to those in our communities who presumably care for us and want what is best for us. They do not ask us to strip down naked and roam the streets, exposing every muddled detail of our personal lives to anyone with two working ears.

As a religion columnist, I too have wrestled with what to reveal and what to guard. A few years ago, I disclosed some of the details of my painful past and early childhood trauma, but I had been having those conversations with my family, friends, and counselor for nearly two years by the time it was published. Even now, I decline many interview requests on the matter, setting boundaries about what personal topics are open for discussion. Looking back, I'm grateful I made the decision to save some details for loved ones only.

In a celebrity age, many people feel they have a right to every intimate detail of other people's lives. But often the ones who demand to know the most are the ones who deserve to know the least.

It is time that people—and especially followers of Jesus—think more seriously about when, what, where, how, and with whom we should share.

It's time we think more intentionally about what *confession* means and should look like in the digital age, in the era of vulnerability.

Confession is both an end and a means to an end. It is a grace, but it also triggers a cascade of grace. When we confess properly and to the right people, a door opens and we step into a new reality, ready to embrace forgiveness, pardon, absolution, liberation. Strangers cannot offer us grace in this way. Only those who know us and love us can.

Reimagining this word, then, requires that we become discerning, which can be an exacting posture to maintain, since no one has written the perfect discernment users' manual. The Bible offers some helpful principles to guide one in such a pursuit, but it doesn't resolve the finer edges.

Though we may yearn for a handbook to navigate life, discernment requires figuring it out in real time. The act of discerning is less like solving a math equation and more like wrestling a crocodile. Mistakes are certain. But the effort of confession and the intention of the confessor both matter.

Take it from someone who has overshared more times than I'd like to admit, often under the banner of "confession": you should think twice before you hit the Submit button. Some experiences and details shouldn't be for sale, no matter how high the bidding.

Often the best way to open one's heart is to close one's mouth.

23

Spirit: Mr. Ghost and the Pronoun Wars

The Emory University professor entered our classroom without a word. Professor Noel Erskine, a brilliant, offbeat scholar from Jamaica, oozed passion and never stopped smiling. Yet on the last day of class he appeared more somber.

"When many of you arrived here, young and full of passion, if someone asked you, 'What is this book?' you would have said, 'That is the word of God,'" he said, holding up a Bible. "But then you took Old Testament survey and New Testament survey and theology, and now they ask you and you don't know anymore."

This was one of the most powerful classroom moments I'd ever witnessed, and I felt a range of emotions circulating around the room and in me.

"You came here to learn about the word of God, and three years later, you go home, and your church doesn't recognize you," he said. "Don't be afraid to believe and proclaim the truth of this book. No matter what you've been told, remember this is God's word."

Liberal colleges claim to be open minded but often suppress conservative viewpoints.[1] I had just been in a class on the book of Romans where the professor railed against the apostle Paul as a misogynistic shyster. An hour later another professor made a rather conservative and exclusivist statement—he said, "*the* word of God." Observing my classmates, I felt proud there was enough grace for that comment to be made at a liberal institution.

My dad used to tell me about the liberal seminary he attended. How he was bullied by professors for his conservative beliefs and shamed for his traditional views. Among his most horrifying stories: one of his professors prayed before class to "Our heavenly Mother."

No wonder I shrunk back whenever I heard anyone speak of God in feminine terms. When the best-selling novel *The Shack* sparked controversy for portraying God as a black woman, I made sure to steer clear. I didn't want to become like those liberal Christians who prayed to "Our heavenly Mother" or like Professor Erskine's students who lost their way and now viewed the Bible as no more divine than *The Hunger Games*.

Masculine images of God and language for God have dominated Western Christianity in Bible translations, hymns, and liturgies. Christian doctrine asserts God is genderless. Yet Christians throughout the centuries still speak of God as male. Which is partly to blame for why so many believe, in the words of one conservative pastor, "God has given Christianity a masculine feel."[2]

After launching my journey to speak God from scratch, I mustered the courage to reevaluate such ideas. One sacred word, *Spirit,* caused me to take another look at gendered language for the Divine.

The word *Spirit* dissolves in the mouth like a communion wafer, by definition immaterial. The words for "Spirit" in Greek, Hebrew, and Latin mean "breath." You exhale the word to speak it. This kind of breath emanates from God and separates the dead from the living.

The apostle John wrote, "God is spirit, and his worshipers must worship in the Spirit and in truth." Jesus said the divine breath blows where it pleases. Though we cannot see God, we glimpse the effects of God. We experience the wonder of God at work in the world. The first chapter of Genesis describes the Spirit hovering across the water; the last chapter of Revelation speaks of the Spirit calling Jesus back.

If you read an English translation of the Bible you might assume the Spirit, *ruach* in Hebrew and *pneuma* in Greek, is masculine. Nope. Translators often attach the male pronoun *he,* but *ruach* is feminine, and *pneuma* is neuter. The word for "Spirit" in Aramaic (the language Jesus spoke) is feminine.

Some say the gender of a noun in Hebrew isn't of much theological significance. After all, gender is assigned to inanimate objects like *table* or *key.* But the Spirit is not an inanimate object. The Spirit is not impersonal. So speaking this word from scratch opens a conversation about considering the feminine attributes of God.

As I've entered into this conversation with friends, many contend that the Bible uses male imagery to speak of God—as a shepherd, king, father, lord, son, and so forth. This is true, but not the whole picture. Consider this:

- The author of Genesis says that both male and female reflect "the image of God."
- The writer of Deuteronomy describes God as a mother eagle, hovering over her offspring, as well as a mother who has just given birth.
- The book of Job speaks of God as having a womb and giving birth to earth's oceans and the frost of heaven.
- In Psalms, God is portrayed as a midwife who attends the delivery of children.
- Isaiah speaks of God as a pregnant woman in labor and as a nursing mother who breastfeeds her children.
- Hosea imagines God as a mama bear that longs for her lost cubs.

- Even Jesus describes himself as a mother hen, who wishes to gather her children under the safety of her wings.[3]

When Christians say they are "born again," they mean that, to borrow Jesus' words, they are "born of the Spirit." Men do not give birth, at least not normally or naturally. Only women do.

"Born again" Christians use feminine language for God even if they don't realize it. They may resist the notion in theory, but the phrase is inherently feminine.

Western Christians are accustomed to thinking about the hands of God and the face of God, but not the womb of God or the breasts of God. Yet the Bible introduces all these metaphors.

When confronted with these examples, some of my friends dig up the goalpost and move it downfield. They counter that throughout its history the church has always opted for masculine language to refer to God.

This turns out to be untrue. Saint Augustine described God as a mother who feeds her earthly infants with heavenly food.[4] The ancient church father Gregory of Narek spoke of God as both "Father Almighty" and "Mother of All." The famous Franciscan writer Anthony of Padua also described God with feminine imagery in the twelfth century, as did Teresa of Avila in the sixteenth century.[5] And the Syriac church has used feminine language to speak of the Holy Spirit for centuries.[6] These images weren't controversial because, unlike us, early Christians didn't treat gender as a wedge issue in a culture war.

Why does this matter to you and me? Because as we've learned, the language we speak shapes us, our emotions, and our thoughts.

In a recent study, people were asked to describe a bridge—a word that is masculine in Spanish and feminine in German. Answers varied according to the respondent's native language. Spanish speakers opted for culturally masculine descriptors like "strong," "sturdy," "towering," and "dangerous." German speakers chose more feminine words such as "beautiful," "elegant," "fragile," "slender," and "pretty."

Those same people were asked to describe a key—a word that is feminine in Spanish and masculine in German—and answers, again, varied. Spanish speakers were more apt to describe a key with adjectives such as "intricate," "little," "lovely," and "shiny." German speakers were more likely to use descriptors like "heavy," jagged," "hard," and "useful."[8]

The result was the same with twenty-four objects in the study. So a word's grammatical gender has serious effects on cognition. Which brings us back to speaking God.

When we only speak of God in masculine language, we can only conceive of God in culturally masculine ways. *Heavy, disciplined, authoritative.* But when we open ourselves up to feminine imagery for God, our minds expand and we imagine God in new ways. *Elegant, intricate, lovely.*[9]

When I was in the eighth grade, I decided to sign up for basketball though I lacked any measure of athletic ability. In order to spend more time with me, my dad decided to serve as assistant coach. As you might imagine, since my #1 fan was coaching, I ended up with the ball more than I deserved.

In the last game of my short-lived career as a power(less) forward, I lobbed a dozen air balls. Exasperated and embarrassed, I broke into tears midcourt. I'll never forget my dad stomping onto the court and wrapping me in his strong arms and telling me that a game was not as important as my heart. In that moment, my father loved me in a way only a father can, and God loves me in that way too.

My mother's love has textures that my father can't provide. When the dark clouds of depression thunder and I need someone to talk to, my mom is the first person I call. When I need a listening ear rather than someone who will fix my problems, I rush to my mother's side. My mother is always willing to give her presence—nurturing and tender, vulnerable and compassionate. God loves me in this way too.

Sometimes I need the love of my father. Other times, only my mother can meet my needs. God is the fullness of love because God is able to give us every shade and expression of love. By including both male and female images in our conceptions of God, we remember that God is the King who reigns as well as the Creator who has birthed us from a loving womb.

> God is the fullness of love because God is able to give us every shade and expression of love.

Male images for God are not inherently dangerous, and they should not be abandoned as some have argued. The problem is when we absolutize these images (or any divine metaphor). Making a single image of God the only way to see God is, in a literal sense, idolatry.[10]

The way we speak of God matters because the way we speak *always* matters. *Spirit* provides us with an opportunity to speak of God with more richness, shades, and depth than we might otherwise. Perhaps we must open our hearts to allow divine breath to blow fresh on us, as we open to the masculine love of our divine Daddy and the warm embrace of the One who gave us birth.

24

Family: Our Changing Households from Munsters to Dunphys

New York City is America's largest city and also our nation's most diverse.[1] Unlike smaller cities and suburbs, the wealthy cannot hide in gated communities far removed from low-income neighborhoods. People from different socioeconomic groups mingle on street corners and café stoops. The borough of Queens is the most linguistically diverse place on planet Earth, with more than eight hundred languages spoken.[2]

Moving to a city of such notable diversity meant encountering all types of people of varying races and religions. No surprise there. But it also meant encountering a wider array of *families* than I had in my previous city of residence—single-parent families, blended families, multiracial families, LGBT families, divorced families, adoptive families, intentionally childless families. In fact, the so-called traditional family might be the minority.

The sprawling bouquet of families in New York City is becoming less of an anomaly than it once was. Communities across America are changing from the inside out. And this can be disconcerting for some people, particularly those who hold to a more conservative value system.[3]

America has morphed in dramatic fashion over the last sixty years, and with it, the word *family*. The number of stay-at-home dads in America has more than doubled over the last decade and a half. Working mothers are now the sole or primary income earners in a record 40 percent of households with children under eighteen.[4] The taboo of adoption is all but gone. And the 2015 Supreme Court's decision legalizing same-sex marriage seems a harbinger of things to come, meaning gay and lesbian parents are increasingly becoming commonplace.

Social conservatives call this transformation the "collapse of the traditional family," but when I began to investigate the word *family* in the modern American conception, I realized there was more to the story. The changes to our understanding of this word are worth unpacking, and one way to examine the shifts is through the lens of American television. After all, TV shows both reflect and shape our culture's values.

"Sometimes pop culture is a reflection of where we are and other times it is a shaping force," says cultural critic Jonathan Fitzgerald. "In the case of television, we often don't know that our morals and values are being shaped until after it happens."[5]

In the 1950s most Americans had a consistent vision for what a family looked like, as television presented a single picture. Popular shows like *Leave It to Beaver* and *Father Knows Best* depicted the family as a heterosexual, patriarchal, Caucasian, churchgoing unit with well-behaved and chaste children.

Depictions of family began morphing during the 1960s, however, and so did our understanding of that word. Strange and spectacular families infiltrated American households. Both *The Addams Family* and *The Munsters* aired from 1964 to 1966, joining the wildly popular *Bewitched*. At first glance, these shows seem to be little more than creative comedies with magical, monster-like characters, but the entertaining storylines were subversive to the ideal family and shattered the Cleaver-family mold. The shows featured traditional families with nontraditional characters. Unbeknownst to most Americans, they provoked a conversation hairier than Cousin Itt: "Can you accept a family that looks different from your own?"

The 1960s also forced audiences to explore the concept of single-parent families, though these households were still patriarchal and resulted from death, not divorce. *The Andy Griffith Show* led the cultural conversation during its nine-year lifespan (joined by *My Three Sons,* which aired until 1972). Through the character of Andy Taylor, a small-town sheriff capable of raising his son, Opie, without the help of a wife, America began wondering whether family could exist without two adult parents. Now considered to be a bastion of traditional values, the show was quietly progressive and helped some Americans whistle a new tune when it came to family.

The 1970s gave us *The Brady Bunch,* conceived after Sherwood Schwartz read in the *Los Angeles Times* that 30 percent of American households included a child from a previous marriage. *The Brady Brunch* broadened Americans' narrow definition of family by demonstrating that fragments of families could be joined together to form a new family. This created a welcoming path for widows and divorcees, who often felt like social pariahs in a traditional society. Viewing audiences accepted this radical redefinition because Mike and Carol's bunch was so relatable and seemingly normal.[6]

African American families rose to television prominence in the 1970s and 80s. Sitcoms like *The Cosby Show* defied American stereotypes of black families as poor and less than. And *The Jeffersons* featured an interracial marriage in the characters of Tom and Helen Willis, just a few years after the 1967 Supreme Court invalidated the laws against such a union.

During the mid to late 1980s, the lead character in *Who's the Boss?,* Tony Micelli, was a single father and former major league baseball player who takes a job working as a live-in nanny and housekeeper for Angela Bower, a single mother and successful business executive. *Who's the Boss?* should've been a scandalous concept because it reversed traditional notions of gender roles. Yet it somehow felt normal to audiences. Though

Angela, Tony, and their children aren't technically related or bound by marriage, it's clear they are a family—and one that's as lovable as they are nontraditional.

Perhaps no show was more unwittingly revolutionary than *Full House,* which aired from 1987 to 1995. News reporter Danny Tanner's wife is killed by a drunk driver, so he enlists his best friend and brother-in-law to help him raise his children. *Full House* is the story of three men successfully raising three girls, and though it seemed totally innocuous, the sitcom opened the door to conversations about same-gender parents.

As America moved into the 1990s, television began exploring the dysfunctions of traditional families. Shows like *Married with Children, Roseanne,* and *The Simpsons* diverge from the *Leave It to Beaver* model by undermining the idea that a family must operate peacefully and smoothly at all times. Despite their controversial nature, audiences gravitated to these shows for more than a decade, perhaps because they saw familiar glimmers of their own families' chaos. *The Simpsons* is America's longest running sitcom.

In the late 1990s and 2000s, television not-so-subtly led Americans into an exploration of issues of sexuality. Ellen Degeneres became famous for playing the first gay or lesbian television character to come out of the closet on air in 1997 and since 2003 has been hosting a popular daytime talk show.[7] And of course, there was the wildly popular *Will & Grace,* whose principal actors made audiences forget they were watching *gay* characters.[8]

In 2009, nearly sixty years of televised conversations about the meaning of *family* came to a head when *Modern Family* debuted to rave reviews. This hit show might be the most progressive show to ever garner such a high level of success because it takes all the nontraditional family elements of the last six decades and crams them into a single sitcom.

Jay and Gloria portray divorcees, a blended family, and a biracial component. Mitchell and Cameron are the gay couple with an adopted child. And Claire and Phil Dunphy provide us with a reversal of traditional gender roles—a strong woman and submissive husband. All of them have at least as much dysfunction as *The Simpsons*. Taken together, *Modern Family* embodies the richly diverse definition of family now held by contemporary Americans.

Yet *Modern Family* doesn't grandstand on controversial issues, and the characters are highly relatable to everyone. This combination— nontraditional elements presented in a nonthreatening way—has potential to reshape cultural opinions and attitudes in profound ways. Like many before it, *Modern Family* is a sitcom about a nontraditional family that really values family.

But all this raises a question that cannot be avoided for those of us who follow Jesus: Which understanding of *family* is the right one? Or, perhaps we might ask, which of these images fit into a Christian notion of family?

Some point back to *Leave It to Beaver,* as if this was what *family* meant and looked like since the beginning of time. This version ignores the many versions of family modeled in the Bible. Which is to say, the "traditional" family isn't all that traditional or universal or even all that biblical.

"Traditional" families are an emotionally supportive unit, with the key bonding mechanism being love, support, and mutual care. *But . . . many families in the Bible are an economically supportive unit, with the key bonding mechanism being provision for the family.*

"Traditional" families are unquestionably monogamous. *But . . . many families in the Bible are polygamous, with God directing and blessing multiple marriages.*[9]

"Traditional" families are small and comprised of, at most, two generations. *But . . . families in the Bible were sprawling and comprised of multiple generations. The average American household numbers around three people, while the average Hebrew household contained between fifty and one hundred.*[10]

"Traditional" families are bound together by a romantic bond. *But . . . families in the Bible are bound together through arrangements that benefit the tribe or increase family standing.*

"Traditional" families place children in a prominent role, often making decisions based on what is best for the youngest members. *But . . . families in the Bible do not highly value children in decision-making or family vision.*

"The 'traditional family' is not a family lifted out of the Bible's patriarchal period, its united kingdom period, its exilic and postexilic period, its early or late New Testament period, or any other period," writes Rodney Clapp. "It is instead a family lifted out of nineteenth-century industrialized Europe and North America."[11]

A pastor friend of mine in New York City recently took me to lunch to talk about how the word *family* had morphed in recent years. A traditionalist, he felt troubled by these changes. He told me that he believed a "biblical family" consisted of one husband who provides for one lovingly submissive wife and some number of obedient children.

"Which family in the Bible do you think is the best model for this?" I asked.

I could see his eyes scanning the pages of the sacred text that he loved so much, searching for an example.

Adam and Eve's children presumably married each other.

Abraham impregnated his slave.

Jacob got tricked into marrying the wrong woman and chose to also wed the one he really wanted. God blessed both marriages and their children.

Moses entered into an interreligious marriage.

David had many wives.

Solomon, whose wisdom is revered by Christians, had a harem of hundreds of concubines.

Hosea married a prostitute—at God's command, no less.

Mary was a teenage bride who had an out-of-wedlock child while betrothed to an older man.

Jesus was a wifeless, childless rabbi.

The apostle Paul was probably single and had complicated views of marriage and family that were controversial at that time.

And all of Jesus' disciples abandoned their homes and any families they had for a traveling ministry. Tradition says that after the Crucifixion, most disciples either died in foreign lands apart from wives and children or were exiled to far off places.

My pastor friend thought and thought, but he couldn't name a single model of a "biblical family" in the entire Bible.

If the Bible is the basis of your notion of family, then an exclusively traditional understanding doesn't work exactly. The Scriptures present a complicated picture of what families look like. In its pages, we encounter a pattern in which God chooses to work through all kinds of families, many that wouldn't be acceptable or even legal in modern America.

Let me be clear: This does not mean that there are not more just or more beneficial forms of family. Every form of family is not equal. But the Bible seems to indicate that God is able and willing to work within a variety of family forms. Accepting this will revolutionize our communities, churches, and politics.

The Bible's most significant contribution to the notion of family is the way it radically redefines the term in a spiritual framework. The primary family bond in the New Testament is the family of God. These bonds are spiritual, rather than genetic or legal. They are neither nuclear in form nor perfect in execution. This family is compromised of a wide array of people unrelated by blood or marriage.

> In the Bible, we encounter a pattern in which God chooses to work through all kinds of families, many that wouldn't be acceptable or even legal in modern America.

It seems that *family* can describe a group of humans who claim each other and are committed to each other and, if Christian, are jointly intent on witnessing to the glory of Christ. They are sometimes related, but sometimes not. Sometimes they include biological children, adopted children, or are childless. Sometimes they're anchored by two parents; sometimes by one or none. The primary couple is sometimes heterosexual, and sometimes not.

All families are complex and complicated, but none are beyond the reach of the Great Parent.

25

Lost: Microaggressions and Our Common Condition

Few words are as seemingly harmless in the hands of religious people as *lost*. What infliction could be loaded into such a miniscule word? We lose socks, our keys, sometimes our minds. Yet Christians often use this term to refer to people who aren't a part of their religious tribe. And this is when the unassuming word *lost* shape-shifts into something else.

"Oh Sara, poor girl. She doesn't know better because she's lost."

"Be patient with Johnny. He's just lost."

"Watch what you say around Tim. He's lost and you may give him the wrong impression of Christians."

I grew up speaking this word in this way too, and I never thought twice about it. That all changed recently when I received an e-mail from a reader who was disgruntled about an article I'd written. He applied the label to me in the same way I'd applied it others in years past.

"After reading your views on the matter, I'm convinced you're lost and need help," he wrote.

Me? Lost? Who do you think you are?!

For the first time in my life, the label was turned back on me. Those four letters stung like an unseen jellyfish.

So I decided to stop and survey this sacred term, beginning with the Bible.

In the gospel of Luke, Jesus offers a trinity of parables on lost-ness. It's his most extensive teaching on the topic. A deep dive into the text reveals the richness of this term as Jesus uses it.

The first story, known as the parable of the lost sheep, tells the story of a shepherd with one hundred sheep. One wanders away. The shepherd leaves the flock to bring the lone woolly critter back into the fold. The second, known as the parable of the lost coin, tells of a woman with ten coins. One slips away. In a frantic hurry, she flips over couch cushions and rugs until the monetary treasure appears.

Often, as Christians, we are taught that the mislaid coin and sheep represent all the people in the world making bad choices. God is the shepherd and the woman in the stories, we assume. When the items are found, it is interpreted as the people being "saved" from further bad choices—presumably by praying a particular prayer and asking Jesus to come into their hearts.

The only problem with this interpretation is that it doesn't seem to fit the story at all. Coins do not sin and neither do sheep. Both are morally neutral objects, and nothing sets them apart from their unlost counterparts. The lost coin is just as shiny as the found ones, and the lost sheep is just as fluffy as the rest of the flock.

Jewish and New Testament scholar Amy-Jill Levine observes, "The shepherd did not expel the sheep for bleating a blasphemy or grazing on non-kosher grass. The sheep did not sin. Rather the shepherd lost the sheep. Similarly, the coin was not cast out; the woman was looking for her money, not divesting from it."[1]

The lost-ness of these items is not the item's fault. Every shepherd knows that *he* is responsible for keeping up with the sheep, and even a child knows that if you lose your moolah, you have no one to blame but yourself. The only reason the sheep is missing is because the shepherd wasn't doing his job. Sheep are pretty defenseless, which is why they need a shepherd. The only reason the coin is missing is because the woman wasn't counting her nickels and dimes.[2] The items are only lost because, well, someone lost them. And they do nothing to be found, either. They are passive objects in the affair. Particularly the coin. It just lies there.

Jesus seems to speak of being lost in a different way than do many who follow his teachings. Lost-ness is the state of being separated from the community and in need of reconciliation, but Jesus does not equate it here with evil or sinfulness. Instead, Jesus gives a sweeping picture of lost-ness that encompasses all who wonder and wander.

Interestingly, Jesus insinuates that when people are "lost," it may not be their fault.

Maybe we are the shepherd and the woman. How often do we take inventory of our communities, and upon identifying those who are now "lost" and disconnected from us, take ownership for the role we may have played in their estrangement? In this view, lost-ness does not quarantine "outsiders" from "insiders." It makes space for "insiders" to own the roles they've played in fracturing community and work to reconcile "outsiders." If religious "insiders" began living that lesson, there would truly be "rejoicing in heaven."

Jesus doesn't stop with flocks and finances. In a common ancient storytelling trick, he sets listeners up with two similar models only to take a surprising, sharp left turn in a third example. Jesus' final story, the parable of the prodigal son, tells of a father with two sons, the younger of whom asks for an early inheritance and then flits off to a faraway land.

We see this story through a Western lens that places a heavy emphasis on individual responsibility, so we naturally blame the departure on the son.

But first-century Jews in a patriarchal, communal culture, would assume the son has been lost by the father. Just as the woman is responsible for keeping track of her money and the shepherd is responsible for his sheep, so too the head male was ultimately responsible for keeping the ancient household together.

After the son leaves, shaming his father, he squanders his inheritance on revelry. Penniless, he must return home and beg for his father's forgiveness. Ancient listeners would assume the boy is heading home to a happy ending. And this is what they get. Well, sort of.

Upon the son's return, the father rejoices and throws him a heckuva shindig with more grade-A choice beefsteak than a hundred lumberjacks could eat. But about the time Jesus' listeners expect a final "The End," Jesus introduces a new character: an elder son. Noting the wayward son has come home, the elder brother is irate. After all, he has followed all the rules and his Pops never gifted him a steak dinner. Jesus flipped the script, and no one saw it coming.

"The father is convinced that the younger, the prodigal, is the one who is lost, and in many respects he is correct," writes Levine. "However, we find out at the end of the parable that the son who is in fact 'lost' is the elder. The owner spots the missing sheep among the hundred, and the woman spots the missing coin among the ten. The father, with only two sons, was unable to count correctly."[3]

Talk about a twist. Not only does Jesus suggest that we may be implicated in someone else's lost-ness, but he adds that the "found" person may in fact be . . . lost as well.

Religious people often use the word *lost* to establish a hierarchy or dividing line, but Jesus uses the term as a bulldozer to level the field.

In this case . . .

The "lost" includes the "outsider" and the "insider."

The "lost" includes the rule breaker *and* the rule follower.

The "lost" includes those who may not even realize they are lost *and* those who wrongly assume they are found.

"Be careful when you assume others are lost and you are not," Jesus seems to be saying. "You may find out that you're actually the one in need of reconciliation and repentance."

A clue that reinforces Jesus' point in this parable occurs in the first story. Jesus explains the end of the parable of the lost sheep: "I tell you that in the same way there will be more rejoicing in heaven over one sinner who repents than over ninety-nine righteous persons who *do not need to repent.*"[4]

That last part seems to be a little Jewish hyperbole. After all, I couldn't locate ninety-nine people who have zero need of repentance if I spent the next ninety-nine years searching for them.

Jesus teaches that some people are lost and need to be found; other people are lost but assume they have already been found. The second group, as Jesus tells it, is worse off.

We all, to some degree and in some way, have wandered away from our true home. Even those who claim to be *saved,* are in some way, still roving. They have been saved, are being saved, and are in need of saving. Sadly, many Christians—myself included—have twisted this word into a broom that we use to sweep others under the rug.

Popularized by sociologist Robert Park, the psychology of marginalization explores the way we think and speak about and treat immigrants, minorities, and those we consider to be immoral.

The telltale sign of marginalization is patronizing behavior. We would never admit that we think we are better than others, but instead we use language to establish a dividing line between "them" and "us." Through *microaggressions* or *microinvalidations,* we communicate that the other is less intelligent or less capable or less enlightened than we are. At first blush, it sounds like we are being compassionate and caring about the sad state of the other. But something else is going on.

Christians have often used the term *lost* in this way, as a microinvalidation. It's a subtly negative term used to refer to "bad" people who, unlike us Christians, need to behave better and accept all the doctrines we believe are true. But Jesus' words in this trio of parables challenges us to reframe our understanding of the word. Maybe this definition is better than ours.

While we often use the term *lost* to refer to someone who needs to get her act together and start following the rules, in these stories, Jesus uses *lost* to mean loved, valuable, and worth pursuing. People who are "lost" are precious, not pitiful.

By playing with the word *lost,* reframing in light of these parables, we can look at the categories that Jesus wants his followers to pursue most fervently: the least, the last, the lost, and the lonely.

He calls us to be the shepherd who places value on the one. In that way, when my e-mailing critic called me "lost," I could appreciate what good company I was in—truly beloved, sought-after company.

I rushed to my computer and sent a quick thank-you note: "I'll take that as a compliment."

In the Beginning Was the Conversation

A mystic friend of mine once told me that life's greatest journeys are cyclical rather than linear. When you end up back where you started, prepare to begin again—only this time, you'll progress with greater wisdom, insight, and courage.

Three years after the wrangler spirit led me to the Iron Wilderness, I had traveled quite a trail. It began with despair, confusion, and silence when I was struck mute in a strange land. The path clarified when I realized that most Americans are also struggling to speak God and that sacred words have been in decline since at least the 1960s. The way forward was charted when my study of linguistics revealed that a posture of wordplay can revive an ailing language. I began implementing this transformative approach in my own life, and now I felt a wind at my back.

One frosty February morning, however, I realized one word I had overlooked. It probably should have been the first term I investigated, but somehow I missed it. The word was, well, *word*.

Since we know that God is something of a linguaphile, we should not be surprised that *word* appears more than six hundred times in the Jewish and Christian Scriptures. The term makes an appearance in almost every book in the sacred library we call the Bible. Among Christians, the standout use of *word* occurs in John's gospel, so I decided to make that home base for my exploration of the term.

The opening of the apostle John's biography of Jesus' life describes Christ this way: "In the beginning was the *Word*, and the *Word* was with God, and the *Word* was God."[1]

Many students of the New Testament have noted how unique it was for the apostle John to nickname Jesus "the Word," or *Logos* in Greek. But after a bit of investigating, I discovered a story that revealed a richness and texture to this term that I'd never before encountered.

In 1466, a bastard boy was born to a priest in Rotterdam, Holland. From the moment he was old enough to read, the child loved literature and Scripture, and his aptitude for both surpassed his passion. The boy learned to read and write classical Latin in grade school. As a young adult, he joined a monastery and later became a scholar.

At birth, the child was given a redundant, if not unfortunate, name: Gerard Gerardson. Fortunately, his birth name was replaced at his christening: Erasmus, which means "beloved."

While Erasmus would become a revered Bible scholar, writing books and lecturing at Cambridge for a time, his most remarkable achievement was translating and publishing the first Greek New Testament with the Latin translation in parallel text. This crowning accomplishment earned him revered status in Christian history.

As Erasmus revised his New Testament translation, the scholar made a revealing decision that most Western Christians have forgotten, to our disadvantage.

When he arrived at the prologue to John's gospel, he grew uneasy. The most popular Latin translation had rendered it with the same phrasing that I encountered in my modern English translation: "In the beginning was the Word, and the Word was with God and the Word was God."

After consulting every relevant source, Erasmus concluded this translation did not accurately capture what the apostle John was trying to communicate.[2] John's chosen word, *Logos,* is complex and dynamic and rarely refers to a single static "word" in Greek literature. *Logos* signifies a continuous statement, an ongoing narrative, a complex utterance in which the audience, not just the speaker, participates.

With determination, an aging Erasmus picked up his pen and rendered this passage more accurately:

> It all arose out of a Conversation,
> Conversation within God, in fact the
> Conversation was God. So, God started the
> discussion, and everything came out of this,
> and nothing happened without consultation.

> This was the life, life that was the light of men,
> shining in the darkness, a darkness which
> neither understood nor quenched its creativity.

> John, a man sent by God, came to remind
> people about the nature of the light so that
> they would observe. He was not the subject
> under discussion, but the bearer of an
> invitation to join in.

> The subject of the Conversation, the original
> light, came into the world, the world that had
> arisen out of his willingness to converse. He
> fleshed out the words but the world did not
> understand. He came to those who knew the
> language, but they did not respond. Those
> who did became a new creation (his children),
> they read the signs and responded.

These children were born out of sharing in
the creative activity of God. They heard the
conversation still going on, here, now, and
took part, discovering a new way of being people.

To be invited to share in a conversation
about the nature of life, was for them, a glorious
opportunity not to be missed.[3]

My eyes widened and my heartbeat quickened as I realized the implications. Thinking of Jesus as a singular word confines us to a one-dimensional understanding of God. It is static and unmovable. But understanding Jesus as a divine Conversation reveals a God who is vibrant, alive, involved, and a good listener.

Jesus didn't just reveal who God is in the past; Jesus reveals who God is in this present moment. That discourse beckons us, draws us, sweeps us up into the Conversation. Which is probably similar to what the apostle Paul meant when he called Christians "a letter from Christ."[4] When we open our mouths and speak God, we are entering into and amplifying the Conversation, participating in divine discourse.

According to some scholars, Erasmus's translation best captured the gospel's message,[5] and yet most English translations reverted back to "Word." What a shame. Because John was trying to tell us that Jesus was not a single word in isolation but rather an ever-expanding and ongoing speech into which we are invited to participate. Speaking God is an excellent calling, "because it was the role God himself has assumed to teach in the voice of flesh the lessons of wisdom."[6]

Jesus is also a reminder that words are not enough. When God wanted to explain what God is like, the explanation took the form of flesh, not just speech. The Incarnation reminds us that we are both liberated and limited by our words.

As Mechthild of Magdeburg, a medieval Christian mystic, said, "Of the heavenly things God has shown me, I can speak but a little word, not more than a honeybee can carry away on its foot from an overflowing jar."

Words can help explain and describe, but only to a point. At some point the Conversation must be wrapped in flesh. If you want to truly describe *grace,* for example, you have to move beyond just speaking about it and start embodying it too. We must learn to live our lexicons. But we can't embody a vocabulary we do not know, understand, or use. And this is where Erasmus helps us along.

Jesus is not just a message from God *to* us. Jesus is also a perpetual call from God *inviting us into* a cosmic conversation. Jesus is a divine reminder that speaking God is worth the wrestling. He is proof that God wants us to keep talking and talking—no matter how fraught with complexities our sacred terms may be.

Learning to speak God from scratch is a cyclical journey rather than linear. Having no beginning or end, the practice is perpetual and perennial. It means participating in the conversation of our ancestors and one our descendants will soon join. The cosmic conversation draws in each new generation of the Jesus way, spiraling us upward and propelling us forward as we peel back new layers of meaning in our most sacred words.

Three years after embarking on my journey to speak God from scratch, I strolled into McCarren Park a few blocks north of my Brooklyn apartment at dusk. I spread a blanket on the lawn and snacked on an array of meats, cheeses, and fruit while I called to mind all the people who had inspired me on my journey.

Sarah was still a college student when she told me that the language of her parents' tradition felt distant from the real world and disconnected from her life experiences. But she didn't give up on faith and wrestled with sacred words instead. She discovered that the vocabulary of faith is less like a dictionary and more like a drawer full of knives—tools that can slice life into more digestible portions of purpose and meaning. Her love for God has now started to take root again.

Bob and his wife had two elementary school–aged children when he entered my life. As a parent, he wished more than anything that his children would embrace God's mysteries. Sacred language plunged him into a sea of frustration as he was met with blank stares. Rather than fall silent, Bob abandoned tired clichés and spoke God from scratch with his kids. He tells me that family devotions and minivan conversations are now fertile ground for fresh spiritual exploration.

Becky was wrestling through midlife when we first met. Disease worried her, suffering confounded her, and the nightly news turned her knees to jelly. Death felt closer than ever. The sacred language she used worked well years ago, but platitudes and praise choruses weren't enough anymore. She started speaking God from scratch, and it revitalized the faith that was once slipping away.

Jerry had been preaching sermons for more years than he'd like to admit, but his altar calls and invitations weren't flooded with people as they once were. Neither were his pews. Every striving for relevance felt fickle and false. He started speaking God from scratch with his parishioners and now says he is seeing fruit from his ministry again.

Speaking God from scratch, like moving to a new city, involves labor pains but results in the birth of new life. My friends weren't the only ones who had matured and morphed. I had too.

I now engaged in spiritual conversations with greater confidence and frequency. Rather than avoid conversations with strangers on the subway, I sought them out. Instead of changing the subject when my barber or my landlord asked me what I did for a living, I stayed the course. Curious taxicab drivers became less of an irritation and more of an opportunity to play with the vocabulary of faith. Over time, I stopped diverting from these topics and began dialoguing about them again. As a result, New York City ceased to be a silence-inducing strange land and is now my spiritual oyster, opening wide and inviting me to explore the richness of sacred terms that gave me life.

My *yes* has been transformed from a common affirmation into a portal for divine possibility. *Creed* has changed from an empty ritual into a life-giving recitation. *Neighbor* is redefined in terms of need rather than near-ness. *Disillusionment* is unmasked as a gift bursting with the power to liberate me from lies I once called truth. *Lost* has stopped being an epithet and has become instead a gentle reminder that when I wander and won-der, I'm in good company. These revelations and others have sparked a heightened awareness of the *Spirit* of God and the surprising ways that God births new creations.

And what about you?

Whether you enter this divine conversation or not is your choice—and only yours. If you choose to say *no,* you'll slam shut the door to sacred speech and save yourself a lot of trouble. If you decide to say *yes*—not denying the obstacles but believing that the struggle is worthwhile—you'll fling open the door to spiritual possibility.

May you say *yes, yes, yes* and keep the fires of sacred speech burning bright.

A How-To Guide for
Seekers and Speakers

You can't learn to speak God from scratch just by reading. You learn by doing. To help you with this task, I've distilled the practice into a simple five-step process. I've called it the **S-P-E-A-K Method** to make it easy to remember.

While this process can work individually, it is best done within the context of community. Invite trusted friends or members of your faith community to join you in this practice.

STOP. Awareness precedes improvement. Before you can speak God more fluently, you must speak God intentionally. This requires stopping and reflecting on tensions you feel.

Gather with your friends or community. Start a new entry in your journals or in the notes section of your smartphones and reflect on any general anxiety you feel about speaking God. Respond to the following three questions in as much detail as possible:

How often do you speak God in a given week?

How many of these spiritual conversations occur in a church setting or in the context of a religious community?

What are the reasons you don't speak God more often?

In addition to general anxiety, it's helpful to stop and consider the specific terms or phrases that are obstacles for you. Human beings speak more than fifteen thousands words on an average day, but we rarely stop to consider the definitions or connotations of the terms themselves. In order to speak God with intentionality, take time to pause and notice the words you are (and are not) using. Return to your journal or smartphone:

Which sacred words do you use but cannot explain without religious jargon?

Which sacred words do you avoid because you don't know what they mean?

Which sacred words make you wince or shrink back due to their negative connotations?

This list is your personal road map for speaking God from scratch. Feel free to add new words as they arise.

PONDER. Consider the words on your list one at a time. Write the *definition* you've ascribed to this word in a precise sentence or two. Then jot down the *connotation* of the word (all the associations this word carries and any emotions its usage triggers).

Once you acknowledge the meaning, it's time to ponder the problems with that meaning. Respond to the following questions in your journal or smartphone:

How has your understanding of this sacred word misrepresented who you believe God is?

How has your understanding of this sacred word inhibited spiritual formation in your life?

How has your understanding of this sacred word contributed to the oppression or discrimination of others?

EXPLORE. As we've learned, it is easy to get stuck in the deconstruction phase. Once you've completed the second step, it is critical that you proceed through a period of reconstruction. Take time to wrestle with fresh ways you might understand each word that would more beautifully represent who God is, contribute positively to your spiritual formation, and avoid harming others.

This is not a totally subjective process. Recall C. S. Lewis's metaphor for language transformation as a tree shooting out new branches (see page 70). The exploration phase should not be a process of *ex nihilo* creation but rather a process of growth or maturation. Take time to explore early meanings of the word in history, in your religious tradition, and in the sacred Scriptures. It may be helpful to search online for the etymology of the word or search a concordance to survey its usage in Scripture. Root yourself here as you explore fresh meanings.

APPLY. Now it is time to engage in what I've called "wordplay." If you've come from a religious tradition that is literalistic or places a heavy emphasis on theological precision, this may feel a little uncomfortable. In this step, you will experiment with your new definition in actual conversations with friends and family, fellow speakers, and maybe even strangers. Explain what you think this word might mean and ask their opinions. If a meaning you've come up with doesn't seem to be working, go back to the previous step and play with the word again. Repeat as necessary.

KEEP TALKING. As linguist Claude Hagège once told the *New York Times,* the future of any language "depends on the will of their speakers to maintain their use."[1] Speaking God from scratch is not an event but a lifelong practice. We must commit to keep talking. Which is to say, to keep struggling, to keep failing, to keep embarrassing ourselves, to keep moving our mouths despite our desire to run like the wind.

Whatever you do, don't give up on trying to speak God. The future depends on speakers like you.

Recommended Reading
for God-Speakers Everywhere

Any geeky linguaphiles like me out there? If so, here is a sampling of books from a range of perspectives that guided me on my journey. They may be meaningful to you too. Happy reading, God-speakers.

Astley, Jeff. *Exploring God-Talk: Using Language in Religion*. Darton, Longman, and Todd, 2004.

Ayto, John. *Dictionary of Word Origins: The Histories of More than 8,000 English-Language Words*. Arcade, 2011.

Borg, Marcus. *Speaking Christian: Why Christian Words Have Lost Their Meaning and Power—And How They Can Be Restored*. HarperOne, 2013.

Buechner, Frederick. *Wishful Thinking: A Seeker's ABC*. Harper & Row, 1973.

Buechner, Frederick. *Whistling in the Dark: A Doubter's Dictionary*. HarperOne, 1993.

Cameron, Averil. *Christianity and the Rhetoric of Empire: The Development of Christian Discourse*. University of California Press, 1991.

Crystal, David. *How Language Works: How Babies Babble, Words Change Meaning, and Languages Live or Die*. Avery, 2007.

Dawn, Marva. *Talking the Walk: Letting Christian Language Live Again*. Brazos, 2005.

Deutscher, Guy. *Through the Language Glass: Why the World Looks Different in Other Languages*. Picador, 2011.

Hallett, Garth L. *Theology Within the Bounds of Language: A Methodological Tour*. SUNY Press, 2012.

Harris, Roy. *Language, Saussure, and Wittgenstein: How to Play Games with Words*. Routledge, 1990.

Hegège, Claude. *On the Death and Life of Languages*. Yale University Press, 2009.

Johnson, Ben. *Godspeech: Putting Divine Disclosures into Human Words.* Eerdmans, 2006.

Kushner, Aviya. *The Grammar of God: A Journey into the Words and Worlds of the Bible.* Spiegel & Grau, 2015.

Lewis, C. S. *Studies in Words.* Cambridge University Press, 2013.

Laubach, Frank Charles. *Learning the Vocabulary of God: A Spiritual Diary.* Martino Fine Books, 1956.

Lischer, Richard. *The End of Words: The Language of Reconciliation in a Culture of Violence.* Eerdmans, 2008.

Matthews, P. H. *Linguistics: A Very Short Introduction.* Oxford University Press, 2003.

McEntyre, Marilyn. *Caring for Words in a Culture of Lies.* Eerdmans, 2009.

McEntyre, Marilyn. *What's In a Phrase: Pausing Where Scripture Gives You Pause.* Eerdmans, 2014.

McFague, Sally. *Metaphorical Theology: Models of God in Religious Language.* Fortress Press, 1982.

McWhorter, John. *The Power of Babel: A Natural History of Language.* Harper Perennial, 2003.

Norris, Kathleen. *Amazing Grace: A Vocabulary of Faith.* Riverhead Books, 1999.

Ostler, Nicholas. *Empires of the World: A Language History of the World.* Harper Perennial, 2006.

Ostler, Nicholas. *Passwords to Paradise: How Languages Have Re-Invented World Religions.* Bloomsbury Press, 2016.

Percy, Walker. *The Message in the Bottle: How Queer Man Is, How Queer Language Is, and What One Has to do With the Other.* Picador, 2000.

Peterson, Eugene. *Tell It Slant: A Conversation on the Language of Jesus in His Stories and Prayers.* Eerdmans, 2012.

Pinker, Steven. *The Stuff of Thought: Language as a Window into Human Nature.* Penguin Books, 2008.

Piper, John and Justin Taylor, ed., *The Power of Words and the Wonder of God.* Crossway, 2009.

Sasso, Sandy Eisenberg. *Midrash: Reading the Bible With Question Marks*. Paraclete Press, 2013.

Soskice, Janet Martin. *Metaphor and Religious Language*. Clarendon Press, 1987.

Spencer, Gregory. *Reframing the Soul: How Words Transform Our Faith*. Leafwood Publishers, 2018.

Stamper, Kory. *Word by Word: The Secret Life of Dictionaries*. Pantheon, 2017.

Taylor, Barbara Brown. *Speaking of Sin: The Lost Language of Salvation*. Cowley, 2001.

Vandermey, Randall. *God Talk: The Triteness and Truth in Christian Cliches*. InterVarsity, 1993.

Wilder, Amos Niven. *Early Christian Rhetoric: The Language of the Gospel*. Baker Academic, 1999.

Williams, Raymond. *Keywords: A Vocabulary of Culture and Society*. Oxford University Press, 1985.

Williams, Rowan. *The Edge of Words: God and the Habits of Language*. Bloomsbury Continuum, 2014.

Wolfe, Tom. *The Kingdom of Speech*. Little, Brown, 2016.

Acknowledgments

Though this book may bear my name, it is not the product of a single individual. It takes a village, as they say, to produce such a work. The fingerprints of countless people are scattered throughout. So I want to offer my gratitude to the many who helped shape this book over the years it took to compose.

This project would not exist, at least not in its current form, without Margaret Feinberg. My mentor, business partner, and a fellow trouble-maker, she supported my work and took time to improve it. The many hours devoted to critiquing, editing, and encouraging me are without price.

Similarly, I thank my dad, who provided fair and necessary critiques of the manuscript. He helped me soften the unnecessarily sharp edges and challenged me to infuse every thought with an extra helping of grace.

My longtime agent, Chris Ferebee, also deserves a heap of credit. He represented me well, pushed me when necessary, and supported my vision for this project. Many thanks to him for being an agent of character, competency, and chemistry—and for being one of my best friends.

As an author and ghostwriter, I've worked with more than a dozen pub-lishing houses, but the team at Penguin Random House, Convergent, and WaterBrook have put them all to shame. I've never worked with a more talented and tireless bunch. Shannon Marchese is an editor who is sober-minded, detail-oriented, and flexible. Douglas Mann, Nicole McArdle, Penny Simon, and Beverly Rykerd were always a step ahead and provided me with all the necessary tools to succeed in terms of pub-licity and marketing. And, of course, this project would not be what it is without Tina Constable and Campbell Wharton, who believed in this project from its inception. I look forward to working with all of you on many more projects.

Thanks to all who joined my launch team and spread the word about this project. You cheered me on when I needed you most and believed in this book before many others. I credit each of you with any marketplace success it achieves.

Thanks to my assistant, Maegan, who helped keep me organized during the editing and promotional phases of this project. Without her, many balls would have been dropped.

Thanks to Barna Group—specifically Roxanne Stone and David Kinnaman—who helped me design and execute a national survey on these issues. Your team's professionalism, hard work, and generosity were indispensible.

Thanks to everyone who reviewed early fragments of this manuscript and provided invaluable feedback: Emma Green, David Dark, John Stackhouse, Annie Downs, Jessica Ritchie, Kate Bowler, Freddy Piumelli, Brenna Noble, Kirsten Powers, Lindsie Yancey, Chandler Epp, Savana Southerland, and Allison Trowbridge.

Also, thanks to Tim Schraeder who provided knowledge on digital marketing and social media. Your expertise and execution is unparalleled. And thanks to Icon Media Group—especially Shannon Stowe—for your incredible publicity efforts.

To all those whom I've forgotten—and I'm sure there are many—grace and gratitude to you.

Notes

0 Struck Mute in a Strange Land

1. Robert P. Jones, "Religious Affiliation of New York Residents by Borough," Public Religion Research Institute, September 22, 2015, www.prri.org/spotlight/religious-affiliation-of-new-york-residents-by-borough/.

2. English professor Jeffrey M. Ringer shares a case study based on a student he calls Eloise, who took a first-year writing course centered on community and civic engagement. Through a series of interviews with Ringer, Eloise revealed that she didn't care what other people thought about her or whether her words offended or annoyed them. She became preachy, pushy, brash, and "regularly offered unsolicited religious advice." Ringer notes that she operated from a "flattened sense of ethos"—that she could back up her beliefs with the Bible was enough. Because Eloise never considered others, she "spoke in ways that alienated her from the class." Thus, her classmates came to see her as just another "narrow-minded rule follower who [was] outspoken, intolerant, moralistic, and staunchly conservative." *Vernacular Christian Rhetoric and Civil Discourse: The Religious Creativity of Evangelical Student Writers* (New York: Routledge, 2016), 122–24.

3. The Barna Group conducted OmniPoll telephone surveys of 1,019 adult Americans. (May 15–19, 2017)

4. Respondents were asked, "Switching to a new topic, have you had a conversation about religion or spirituality with anyone in the last year? If so, how many times?"

1. Sacred Words in Crisis

1. David Brooks, "What Our Words Tell Us," *The New York Times*, May 20, 2013, www.nytimes.com/2013/05/21/opinion/brooks-what-our-words-tell-us.html.

2. Pelin Kesebir and Selin Kesebir, "The Cultural Salience of Moral Character and Virtue Declined in Twentieth Century America," *Journal of Positive Psychology,* 7, no. 6 (November 2012), www.tandfonline.com/doi/abs/10.1080/17439760.2012.715182.

3. Marcus Borg, *Speaking Christian: Why Christian Words Have Lost Their Meaning and Power—And How They Can Be Restored* (New York: HarperCollins, 2011), 9.

4. William Graham Sumner, *Folkways: A Study of the Sociological Importance of Usages, Manners, Customs, Mores, and Morals* (Boston: Ginn & Co., 1911), 14.

5. Frank Lambert, *Religion in American Politics* (Princeton, NJ: Princeton University Press, 2008).

6. Jonathan Merritt, *A Faith of Our Own: Following Jesus Beyond the Culture Wars* (New York: Hachette, 2012), 33.

7. Danielle Campoamor, "My Christianity Has Failed Me & I Won't Let It Fail My Son," www.romper.com/p/my-christianity-has-failed-me-i-wont-let-it-fail-my-son-34097.

8. Amelia Thomson DeVeaux, "Millennials Leave Their Church Over Science, Lesbian and Gay Issues," PPRI, October 6, 2011, www.prri.org/spotlight/millennials-leave-their-churches-over-science-lesbian-gay-issues/.

9. "Student Banned from Writing About God as 'Hero,'" WRCB, October 18, 2013, www.wrcbtv.com/story/23727459/student-banned-from-writing-about-god-as-hero.

10. I am not the kind of Christian who believes Americans have chased God out of public schools. I do not support reinstating teacher-led prayer in classrooms, and I believe it is a violation of the establishment clause of the US Constitution when public-school teachers and administrators favor Christian students, even in veiled ways.

11. One of the perceived evils among young people is to sound intolerant, bigoted, or narrow-minded. It makes sense, then, that a fear of coming across as someone who holds fundamentalist or intolerant beliefs (something often associated with religion while they were coming of age) would turn them away from the topic altogether.

12. See also Jonathan Merritt, "Are Conservative Christians 'Religious Extremists'?" *The Atlantic,* March 2016, www.theatlantic.com /politics/archive/2016/03/ are-conservative-christians-religious-extremists/473187/.

13. I first encountered this image in Bobette Buster, *Do Story* (London: Do Book Company, 2013). In her book, she imagines the fire as a metaphor for storytelling.

14. J. Robert Wright, *They Still Speak: Readings for The Lesser Feasts* (New York: Church, 2000) 151.

15. Southern Poverty Law Center, "Jonathan Daniels" profile, www .splcenter.org/what-we-do/civil-rights-memorial/civil-rights-martyrs /jonathan-daniels. See also Mary Frances Schjonberg, "Remembering Jonathan Daniels 50 Years After His Martyrdom," Episcopal News Service, August 13, 2015, http://episcopaldigitalnetwork.com /ens/2015/08/13/remembering-jonathan-daniels-50-years-after-his -martyrdom/.

2. Why Speaking God Matters

1. John Horrigan, "Libraries at the Crossroads," Pew Research Center, September 15, 2015, www.pewinternet.org/2015/09/15/libraries -at-the-crossroads/.

2. This transformation means that libraries now serve as a great leveler by providing access to technology and information to those at the bottom of the socioeconomic ladder. (Remember, the internet is not free.)

3. These are common elements of language found in various sources, but they are also three of the elements listed as crucial to religious formation in Nicholas Ostler, *Passwords to Paradise: How Languages Have Re-Invented World Religions* (London: Bloomsbury, 2016), xix.

4. The idea that language shapes thought is not altogether new. In the 1930s, an American linguist named Benjamin Lee Whorf argued that one's language prevents one from being able to think certain thoughts and influences us to think others. His hypothesis dazzled

scholars and the general public, but ultimately could not overcome one big problem: a lack of evidence to back it up. When Whorfism failed, linguists like Noam Chomsky began to propose that language and thought were universal. But more than seventy years after Whorf, the emerging evidence has shown that language does in fact influence our thinking.

5. Lera Boroditsky, "How Language Shapes Thought," *Scientific American* (February 2011), www.scientificamerican.com/article /how-language-shapes-thought/. Additionally, she notes that people who think about directions are better at keeping track of where they are geographically than people who speak other languages.

6. Lera Boroditsky, "Lost in Translation," *The Wall Street Journal,* July 23, 2010, www.wsj.com/articles/SB10001424052748703467304575383131592767868.

7. I have different words for green and blue as an English speaker, but other languages consider them shades of a single color. At the same time, my native language only has a single word for blue while some languages, like Russian, have different words for different shades. As a result, the brains of those who speak languages that treat colors as distinct are trained to exaggerate the differences between these colors.

   Because we speak differently, we see differently. If I, as an English speaker, take a Russian-speaking friend to the Metropolitan Museum of Art, we will have different experiences looking at the same works of art. We have different conceptions of colors. When I stare at Monet's *Water Lilies,* I may notice different lines and shades than my Russian-speaking friend. And he may note features that I have overlooked.

8. Boroditsky, "Lost in Translation."

9. Jessica Gross, "How Language Can Affect the Way We Think," TED, February 19, 2013, http://ideas.ted.com/5-examples-of-how -the-languages-we-speak-can-affect-the-way-we-think/.

10. Boroditsky, "How Language Shapes Thought."

11. Keith Chen, "Saving for a Rainy Day," TED, February 19, 2013, http://blog.ted.com/saving-for-a-rainy-day-keith-chen-on-language-that-forecasts-weather-and-behavior/. As well, new research shows that we process ethics differently and make different moral judgments based on which language a moral dilemma is presented in; see Julie Sedivy, "How Morality Changes in a Foreign Language," *Scientific American,* September 14, 2016, www.scientificamerican.com/article/how-morality-changes-in-a-foreign-language/.

12. Steven Pinker, *The Stuff of Thought: Language as a Window into Human Nature* (New York: Penguin Books, 2008), 22–23.

13. Gregory Spencer, *Reframing the Soul: How Words Transform Our Faith,* (Abilene, TX: Leafwood, 2018), 21.

3. Our Divine Linguaphile

1. Actually, saying that God is a linguaphile may not go quite far enough. It is not just that God has an *affection* for language but also an *aptitude* for language. God possesses what Germans call a *sprachgefühl,* which translates into English as a "feel for language." Words are woven into God's DNA—they are part of who God is.

2. According to David Crystal, "We cannot call 'animal communication' language. The facial expressions, gestures, and tactile behaviours of the animal kingdom lack productivity and duality of structure in the same way that human body language does." *How Language Works* (New York: Avery, 2005), 9–10.

3. Darwin recognized how special language seemed to be. In his last years, he did his best to spin a story about how language could have emerged from song birds. The evidence was so lacking that it embarrassed him to the point where his reputation almost never recovered. History has tried to forget the book in which Darwin published the idea. For a full discussion of this, see Tom Wolfe, *Kingdom of Speech* (New York: Little, Brown, 2016).

4. Marc D. Hauser et al., "The Mystery of Language Evolution," *Frontiers in Psychology,* May 7, 2014, www.frontiersin.org/articles/10.3389/fpsyg.2014.00401/full.

5. Reynolds Price, *A Palpable God* (New York: Atheneum, 1978), 3.
6. Barbara Brown Taylor, "Worthless Religion" (sermon, Duke Chapel, September 2012). Taylor is actually commenting on James 1:18 in which the writer picks up on this Jewish idea connecting words to human creation: "[God] chose to give us birth through the word of truth, that we might be a kind of firstfruits of all he created."
7. Walter Bruggemann, *Texts That Linger, Words That Explode: Listening to Prophetic Voices* (Minneapolis: Augsburg Fortress: 2000), 3.
8. Proverbs 18:21
9. Proverbs 12:18
10. Barbara Brown Taylor, *Gospel Medicine* (Cambridge, MA: Cowley, 1995), 4.
11. Matthew 12:36–37; Matthew 15:18; Mark 11:22–24; Luke 6:45
12. Acts 4:20, NRSV
13. In *Reframing the Soul,* Gregory Spencer says that when Paul repeatedly asks, "What shall we *say?*" (emphasis mine) he is demonstrating the "language attentiveness" of Jesus. "In each instance, he implies, 'Should we continue telling ourselves error? No, we should speak the truth. We should live the truth.'" (29–30).
14. This is true of any religious tradition. As Nicholas Ostler says, "Practice of a religion presupposes use of a language." *Passwords to Paradise* (London: Bloomsbury USA, 2016).

4. The Possibility of Revival

1. Part of the disagreement stems from how to group "families" of languages. For a good discussion of this, see Stephen R. Anderson, "How Many Languages Are There in The World," Linguistic Society of America, www.linguisticsociety.org/content/how-many -languages-are-there-world.
2. John Noble Wilford, "World's Language Dying Off Rapidly," *The New York Times,* Sept. 18, 2007. www.nytimes.com/2007/09/18 /world/18cnd-language.html.

3. Ben Schott, "Q and A: The Death of Languages," *The New York Times,* December 16, 2009, http://schott.blogs.nytimes.com/2009/12/16/q-and-a-the-death-of-languages/?_r=0.

4. SBS News, "Linguicide: How Dying Languages Kill Multiculturalism," www.sbs.com.au/news/linguicide-how-dying-languages-kill-multiculturalism.

5. For more on the causes of language death, see Claude Hagège, *On the Death and Life of Languages* (New Haven: Yale University Press, 2011), 75–168.

6. Hagège, *On the Death and Life of Languages,* 116–17.

7. See "When a Language Dies, What Happens to Culture?" NPR, June 18, 2013, www.npr.org/2013/06/18/193135997/when-a-language-dies-what-happens-to-culture. See also Hagège, *On the Death and Life of Languages,* 131–35.

8. It's nearly impossible to estimate this number with accuracy, but this number may actually be too conservative. LifeWay's Thom Rainer recently estimated the actual number may be eight thousand to ten thousand annual church closings. See Rainer, "13 Issues for Churches in 2013," Church Leaders, January 15, 2013, www.churchleaders.com/pastors/pastor-articles/164787-thom-rainer-13-issues-churches-2013.html.

9. Toni Ridgaway, "Statistics Don't Tell the Whole Story When It Comes to Church Attendance," Church Leaders, October 7, 2013, www.churchleaders.com/pastors/pastor-articles/170739-statistics-don-t-tell-the-whole-story-when-it-comes-to-church-attendance.html.

10. Kelly Shattuck, "7 Startling Facts: An Up Close Look at Church Attendance in America," Church Leaders, https://churchleaders.com/pastors/pastor-articles/139575-7-startling-facts-an-up-close-look-at-church-attendance-in-america.html.

11. Lera Boroditsky, "How Language Shapes Thought," *Scientific American,* February 2011.

12. K. David Harrison, *When Languages Die: The Extinction of the World's Languages and the Erosion of Human Knowledge* (New

York: Oxford University Press, 2007), 3. For more on this, see Hagège, *On the Death and Life of Languages.*

13. Jack Fellman, *The Revival of Classical Tongue: Eliezar Ben Yehuda and the Modern Hebrew Language* (Berlin: Walter de Gruyter, 1973), 137.

14. "Yiddish on the Rise," *The Economist,* July 2015, www.economist.com/blogs/prospero/2015/07/jewish-culture and Jared Samilow, "Yiddish is Making a Comeback – and for Good Reason," Haaretz, February 2016, www.haaretz.com/jewish/the-jewish-thinker/.premium-1.702533.

15. Hagège, *On the Death and Life of Languages,* 330.

16. Claire Felter, "Can We Revive Endangered Languages? Should We?" *The Christian Science Monitor,* March 2015, www.csmonitor.com/Science/Science-Notebook/2015/0324/Can-we-revive-endangered-languages-Should-we.

5. How (Not) to Speak God

1. I'm an Enneagram 3. Go figure.

2. Etymologies have complex histories and nuanced meanings, but as Jim Rader says, "Few of us want to live with these complexities." Quoted in Kory Stamper, *Word by Word: The Secret Life of Dictionaries* (New York: Pantheon, 2017), 188.

   According to Raymond Williams: "This raises one of the theoretical problems. It is common practice to speak of the 'proper' or 'strict' meaning of a word by reference to its origins. . . . The original meanings of words are always interesting. But what is often most interesting is the subsequent variation." *Keywords: A Vocabulary of Culture and Society* (Oxford: Oxford University Press, 2014), xxxii.

   According to Stamper: "It is easy to assume that no matter how convoluted and ridiculous English seems to be today, it can be straightforward and logical if we trace it back to its beginnings. It's a beguiling idea: that there's a golden plumb line of logic that English follows, and we just need to snag it to unravel the mysteries of the language." *Word by Word,* 172.

But even etymology itself isn't fixed and is rooted in conjecture. As new scholarship emerges, our understanding of a word's history morphs. See Stamper, *Word by Word, 175.*

3. This story is paraphrased from 2 Kings 20:12–15. The paraphrase is taken from my book *A Faith of Our Own: Following Jesus Beyond the Culture Wars* (Nashville: FaithWords, 2012).

4. 2 Kings 20:16–18

5. 2 Kings 20:19, emphasis mine.

6. Jonathan Merritt, "Is 'God' a Trigger Word," Buzzfeed, October 22, 2015, www.buzzfeed.com/jonathanmerritt/god-a-trigger-word ?utm_term=.dt1K4YoQxJ#.kgq4DeJ9d7.

7. Christians aren't the only ones who opt for *substitution*. Not far from where Bell spoke that night in Manhattan, the Lab/Shul Jewish community had recently adopted a "BYOG" approach: "Bring Your Own God." A note from the community's leader explained they are committed to "replacing the baggage-laden word 'God' with several other names and prisms that enable us to better connect with and describe the inherently indescribable." See Merritt, "Is 'God' a Trigger Word."

8. Merritt, "Is 'God' a Trigger Word."

9. The language of faith, like all languages, derives from the communities that speak it. The words I hear in my liturgical Manhattan congregation are often different from the ones we spoke back in my contemporary church in Georgia or the ones I hear when I visit my friend's house church in Portland, Oregon. We use many of the same words, of course, but often the definitions we apply to them vary widely. When my Catholic friends use the word *baptism,* they imagine a baby having water poured on her head. When my Baptist friends use it, they picture an adult being dunked in a pool. And when my Pentecostal friends say that word, they often think of encountering the Holy Spirit, dancing in aisles, being healed of diseases, and speaking in tongues. This variation can create the kind of confusion that can drive the death of a language. See Barbara Brown Taylor,

Speaking of Sin: The Lost Language of Salvation (Lanham, MD: Cowley, 2001), 1–3.

10. From a personal interview with Kelly in 2017. Similarly, author Brian McLaren notes that growing numbers are starting to awaken to the destructive concepts tied to spiritual words. He writes, "We are coming to see that in hallowed words like *almighty, sovereignty, kingdom, dominion, supreme, elect, chosen, clean, remnant, sacrifice, lord,* and even *God,* dangerous viruses often lie hidden, malware that must be identified and purged from our software if we want our future to be different from our past." *The Great Spiritual Migration: How the World's Largest Religion is Seeking a Better Way to Be Christian* (New York: Convergent Books, 2017), 90.

11. See "New Persuasive Words for Defaced or Degraded Ones: Mercy, Grace, and Hope in an Age of Recession," Mockingbird, July 20, 2010, www.mbird.com/2010/07/now-available-new-persuasive -words-dvd/. I also highly recommend pastor Paul Zahl's series of talks on the matter, which can also be found at this website.

12. David Crystal, *How Language Works: How Babies Babble, Words Change Meaning, and Languages Live or Die* (New York: Penguin, 2005), 232.

13. Stamper, *Word by Word,* 241–42.

14. Martin, quoted in Merritt, "Is 'God' a Trigger Word."

15. Sally McFague, *Metaphorical Theology: Models of God in Religious Language* (Minneapolis: Fortress Press, 1982).

16. To wit: "A living language *must* change, or die. Most obviously, its vocabulary and meanings change in response to the changing needs of its speakers and the different ways they live their lives," *Heinemann English Dictionary,* 2001, xxii; "The fact is that all languages change over time for a variety of reasons," Anita K. Barry, *Linguistic Perspectives on Language and Education* (Portsmouth, NH: Greenwood , 2002), 84; "All languages change over time and distinct varieties of a language may develop in the different regions

where it is spoken," Keith Allan, ed., *The Routledge Handbook of Linguistics* (London: Routledge, 2015), 7; "If a language does not change, it becomes stagnant and dies," Jean Aitchison, *Language Change: Progress or Decay* (Cambridge: Cambridge University Press, 2001); "All languages change over time, and many aspects of language can change, including the boundaries between words," Carol Genetti, *How Languages Work* (Cambridge: Cambridge University Press, 2014),74; "All languages change over time. Language is not *static;* it is *dynamic.* It doesn't 'run in place;' it constantly changes as the years go by," Harriet Luria, Deborah M. Seymour, and Trudy Smoke, eds., *Language and Linguistics in Context* (Routledge, 2012), 129. One of the world's foremost experts on language, David Crystal says, "However language began, one thing is certain—it immediately began to change, and has been changing ever since. Languages are always in a state of flux. . . . Language purists do not welcome it, but they can do very little about it. Language would stand still only if society did. A world of unchanging linguistic excellence, based on the brilliance of earlier literary forms, exists only in fantasy. The only languages that do not change are the dead ones." *How Language Works,* 357.

17. C. S. Lewis, *Studies in Words* (Cambridge: Cambridge University Press, 2013), 8.
18. Peter J. Schakel and Charles A. Huttar, *Word and Story in C. S. Lewis: Language and Narrative in Theory and Practice* (Wipf and Stock, 2008), 32.
19. Schakel and Huttar, *Word and Story,* 32.
20. Based on your upbringing, this may all feel squishy. Let me try to put you at ease. Language shifts do not place meaning in the eye of the beholder. Definitions matter, and dictionaries are still useful. I don't believe that any word can mean anything you want it to. If a word can mean anything, then a word means nothing. Red cannot suddenly mean blue, just because you don't like fire engines.

6. *The Way Forward*

1. Emphasis added.
2. Deuteronomy 6:5; c.f. Matthew 22:37, Luke 10:27
3. We are probably the most literalistic people who've ever walked the earth. The word corresponds to a single reality—only one at one time. But this isn't at all like the ancients who saw double, triple, or more meanings; see Sally McFague, *Metaphorical Theology: Models of God in Religious Language* (Minneapolis: Fortress, 1982), 5.
4. Claire Felter, "Can We Revive Endangered Languages? Should We?" *The Christian-Science Monitor,* March 2015, www.csmonitor .com/Science/Science-Notebook/2015/0324/Can-we-revive -endangered-languages-Should-we.
5. Gary Eberle, *Dangerous Words: Talking about God in an Age of Fundamentalism* (Boulder, CO: Shambhala, 2007), 50.
6. In 1806, Noah Webster published his first reference with the name *A Compendious Dictionary of the English Language.* By the 1800s, the whole English-speaking world had shifted, sweeping up all sectors of society. Americans became obsessed with dictionaries and the power they held, which led to *Merriam-Webster's Collegiate Dictionary* becoming the second-best-selling book in history, bested only by the Bible.
7. Kory Stamper, *Word by Word: The Secret Life of Dictionaries* (New York: Knopf Doubleday, 2017), 12.
8. David Crystal, *How Language Works: How Babies Babble, Words Change Meaning, and Languages Live or Die* (New York: Penguin Group, 2005), 210.
9. "Some people, when they see a word, think the first thing to do is define it. Dictionaries are produced and, with a show of authority no less confident because it is so limited in place and time, what is called a proper meaning is attached. . . . [This allows us to] appropriate a meaning which fitted the argument and to exclude those meanings which were inconvenient to it. . . . But for words of a different kind, and especially for those which involve ideas and

values, it is not only an impossible but irrelevant procedure. The dictionaries most of us use, the defining dictionaries, will in these cases, and in proportion to their merit as dictionaries, list a range of meanings, all of them current, and it will be the range that matters. Then when we go beyond these to the historical dictionaries, and to essays in historical and contemporary semantics, we are quite beyond the range of 'proper meaning.' We find a history and complexity of meanings; conscious changes or consciously different uses; innovation, obsolescence, specialization, extension, overlap, transfer; or changes which are masked by normal continuity so that words which seem to have been there for centuries, with continuous general meanings, have come in fact to express radically different or radically variable, yet sometimes hardly noticed meanings and implications of meaning." Raymond Williams, *Keywords: A Vocabulary of Culture and Society* (Oxford: Oxford University Press, 2014), xxviii–xxix.

10. Stamper, *Word by Word,* xii; Stamper also notes that the creation of a dictionary is not a once-and-done process. As soon as a lexicographer explains how a word is used, a new sense of the word emerges or a new word appears or a word slides from one part of speech to another. As soon as a dictionary is printed, it is to some degree antiquated. So the goal of lexicographers is to craft a definition that is precise enough to include the common usage but also broad enough that it will hopefully fit the emerging uses of the word.

11. Stamper, *Word by Word,* 95.

12. Stamper, *Word by Word,* 96.

13. As English scholar Gary Eberle notes, "This new attitude toward language—that the ideal text should have a single meaning that should be fixed and immutable for all time—was inevitably applied to religious language, even scripture," *Dangerous Words,* 51.

14. For a more complete list, see Jeff Astley, *Exploring God-Talk: Using Language in Religion* (Darton, Longman and Todd, 2004), 40–41.

15. Jonathan Merritt, "God as a Wild Dog . . . And the Bible's Other Surprising Divine Metaphors," Religion News Service, March 2015, http://religionnews.com/2015/03/25/god-wild-dog-bibles-others-surprising-divine-metaphors/.

16. Sally McFague, *Metaphorical Theology: Models of God in Religious Language* (Minneapolis: Fortress Press, 1987).

17. As Martin Buber once wrote, "Every man of Israel is told to think of himself as standing at Mount Sinai to receive the Torah. For man there are past events and future events, but not so for God: day in, day out, he gives the Torah." *The Way of Man and Ten Rungs* (New York: Citadel Press, 2006), 81.

18. Astley, *Exploring God-Talk*, 45.

19. For thoughts on the benefits of indirect communication when speaking God, see Kierkegaard's theory of communication and thoughts on indirect communication.

20. As New Testament scholar Peter Enns says, "All the examples of biblical interpretation we look at from the Second Temple period, including the New Testament, are midrashic." *Inspiration and Incarnation: Evangelicals and the Problem of the Old Testament* (Ada, MI: Baker Academic, 2015), 188. To see examples of how this actually works, see James Kugel, *In Potiphar's House: The Interpretive Life of Biblical Texts* (Harvard: Harvard University Press, 1994).

21. John Renard, *Fighting Words* (Oakland: University of California, 2012), 5–9.

22. Theologian Dan Cupitt writes, "If we look at any canonical list of mystics, what one notices straightaway is that they are writers, wordsmiths. Not reporters but writers. . . . What they write is best interpreted as a slightly mocking and subversive commentary upon the officially approved forms of words for speaking about God." Quoted in Astley, *Exploring God-Talk*, 15.

23. Kathleen Norris, *Amazing Grace* (New York: Riverhead Books, 1998), 360. "Since the earliest days of the Christian church, there has been a curious tension between Semitic storytelling,

which admits a remarkable diversity of voices, perspectives, and experiences into the canon, and Greek philosophy, which seeks to define, distinguish, pare down." Norris, *Amazing Grace,* 359–60.

24. Walter Brueggemann, *From Whom No Secrets Hid: Introducing the Psalms* (Louisville, KY: Westminster John Knox, 2014), xii.

25. N.T. Wright, *Scripture and the Authority of God* (New York: HarperCollins, 2011), 23.

26. Richard Rohr, "Order, Disorder, Reorder," Center for Action and Contemplation, February 2016, https://cac.org/order-disorder -reorder-2017-07-14/.

27. Richard Rohr has acknowledged the first two stages as hang-ups for conservatives and progressives, respectively. https://cac.org /order-disorder-reorder-2016-02-23/.

28. Reynolds Price, *A Palpable God* (San Francisco: North Point Press, 1985), 6.

7. Yes: Sacred Affirmations and Necessary Nos

1. Reynolds Price, *A Palpable God* (San Francisco: North Point Press, 1985), 54.

2. Kathleen Norris, *Amazing Grace* (New York: Riverhead Books, 1998), 1.

3. 2 Corinthians 1:19

4. My writing mentor, Margaret Feinberg, and I have taught this principle to hundreds of students through our Write Brilliant seminars, and it never fails to deepen and enhance their writing.

5. Richard Rohr, *The Naked Now* (New York: Crossroad, 2009), 51.

6. The "necessary no" is developed by Richard Rohr in his book *The Naked Now* (Crossroad, 2009).

7. E. Stanley Jones, *The Divine Yes* (Nashville: Abingdon, 1975).

8. Creed: Heresy Hunters and Twitter Farewells

1. John Ayto, *Dictionary of Word Origins* (New York: Arcade Books, 2011), 280.

2. *Oxford English Dictionary*, s.v. "heresy."

3. Kate Bolick, *Spinster: Making a Life of One's Own* (New York: Crown, 2015), 18n.

4. The word *heresy* began to decline in English literature around the mid-1800s, but according to a Google Ngram search of *heretic, heresy,* and *heretical,* the decline leveled off in the 1970s, when certain religious sects began recovering it. This seems to support the notion that these words have been revived in certain communities in recent years, even though the broader society isn't using them often.

5. Austin Fischer, "White Heresy, Black Heresy," *Patheos* (blog), November 5, 2015, www.patheos.com/blogs/jesuscreed/2015/11/05/white-heresy-black-heresy-by-austin-fischer/.

6. Justin Holcomb, *Know the Heretics* (Grand Rapids, MI: Zondervan, 2014), 17. Part of the problem, according to Holcomb, is that many people confuse heresy with heterodoxy. The first word is a belief that denies a teaching officially defined as orthodoxy while the second is a belief that diverges from commonly accepted teaching.

7. Tony Jones, "It's Time for a Schism Regarding Women in the Church," *Patheos,* November 2013, www.patheos.com/blogs/tonyjones/2013/11/22/its-time-for-a-schism-regarding-women-in-the-church/.

8. Alister McGrath, *Heresy: A History of Defending the Truth* (repr., New York: HarperOne, 2010).

9. Justin S. Holcomb, "Why You Shouldn't Call That False Teaching a Heresy," *Christianity Today,* October 6, 2015, www.christianitytoday.com/ct/2015/october/truth-about-heresy.html. See also Jonathan Merritt, "Who's Afraid of a Big, Bad Heretic? An Interview with Justin Holcomb," Religion News Service, June 16, 2014, http://religionnews.com/2014/06/16/heretics-christians-justin-holcomb/.

10. Interestingly, the earliest Christians defined *orthodoxy* firstly as right worship and only secondarily as correct doctrine. While most people today think of orthodoxy as a rigid set of doctrinal

points, that definition does not become dominant in Western Christianity until the mid-sixteenth century, when reeling Catholic churches and infant Protestant congregations sought to codify their doctrines in order to differentiate their brand of Christianity from the rest. Aidan Kavanagh, *On Liturgical Theology* (Collegeville, MN: Pueblo Books, 1984), 3. See also Kathleen Norris, *Amazing Grace*, 209–210.

11. Helmut Thielicke, *The Trouble with the Church* (London: Hodder & Stoughton, 1966), 40.

9. Prayer: Folded Hands and Brain Scans

1. I thought this practice was innovative at the time, but I now know it is centuries old. (Related to this, early Christians might ask another to "give me a word" in order to assist her in her spiritual journey. The phrase has survived among many Christians today.)

2. Jonathan Merritt, "This Is Your Brain on Religion," *Relevant*, April 16, 2013, http://archives.relevantmagazine.com/god/practical-faith /your-brain-religion.

3. Merritt, "This Is Your Brain on Religion."

4. Merritt, "This Is Your Brain on Religion."

5. Romans 1:20

10. Pain: Chronic Conditions and Other Metaphors

1. "Chronic pain costs U.S. up to $635 billion, study shows," *Science Daily*, Sept. 11, 2012.

11. Disappointment: Dopamine Roller Coasters and Palm Branches

1. Maia Szalavitz, "The Chemistry of Addiction Explains Why Disappointment Hurts So Badly By," *New York*, November 9, 2016.

2. Szalavitz, "Why Disappointment Hurts So Badly."

3. See Matthew 21, NRSV; Mark 11; Luke 19; and John 12.

4. They are coming from Jericho, the lowest city on planet Earth at more than 800 feet below sea level. Their destination is Jerusalem, which is only about fifteen miles away but is 3,000 feet above sea

level. Each step seems to inject the story with anticipation. The road
finally reaches its peak at the Mount of Olives, where the Rabbi
and his followers look out over all of Jerusalem, where the Passover
feast is kicking off. There a dull roar bounces off the mountainsides
because, during Passover, this city of about 40,000 swells to
400,000 or more. Imagine the 1.6 million residents of Manhattan
rising to 16 million for a week, or envision your community
expanding tenfold overnight. Jerusalem was a zoo.

5. C.S. Lewis, *The Problem of Pain* (New York: Harper One, 2015), 91.
6. C. S. Lewis, *A Grief Observed* (New York: HarperOne, 2001), 6–7.
7. Barbara Brown Taylor, *God in Pain* (Nashville: Abingdon Press, 1998), 20.

13. *God: Tattooed Jesus and a Full-Narrative Deity*

1. "American Piety in the 21st Century: New Insights to the Depth
and Complexity of Religion in the US: Selected Findings from The
Baylor Religion Survey, September 2006," Baylor.edu, www.baylor
.edu/content/services/document.php/33304.pdf. I first encountered
this study in Christian Piatt's *postChristian*, (New York: Little,
Brown, 2014), 149–52, where it was listed along with related and
equally fascinating data. Piatt also frames this data in the broader
context of religious-based fear, which I find a helpful addition to
this conversation.
2. Ross Pomeroy, "Belief in Angry God Associated with Poor Mental
Health," *Real Clear Science*, April 16, 2013, www.realclearscience
.com/blog/2013/04/belief-in-punitive-god-associated-with-poor
-mental-health.html.
3. Warren Throckmorton, "How the Religious Right Scams Its Way
onto the New York Times Bestseller List," *Daily Beast*, November
16, 2014, www.thedailybeast.com/how-the-religious-right-scams
-its-way-onto-the-new-york-times-bestseller-list.
4. Kristen Powers, "Why is a popular interfaith website giving a
disgraced misogynistic pastor a platform?" *The Washington Post*,
October 20, 2017, www.washingtonpost.com/news/acts-of-faith

/wp/2017/10/20/why-is-a-popular-interfaith-website-giving-a
-disgraced-misogynistic-pastor-a-platform/?utm_term=.1f455ebb
67d7 and Marc Cortez, "Stay-at-home dads should be disciplined
by the church," *Everyday Theology,* October 28, 2010, http://
marccortez.com/2010/10/28/.

5. Lauren Sandler, "The pastor's wife made him do it," Salon.com.
November 7, 2006. www.salon.com/2006/11/07/driscoll/.

6. See Matthew Paul Turner, *Our Great Big American God: A Short
History of Our Ever-Growing Deity* (New York: Jericho), 2014.

7. Mark Driscoll, quoted in "7 Big Questions: Seven Leaders on
Where the Church Is Headed," *Relevant,* October 13, 2007, http://
web.archive.org/web/20071013102203/http://relevantmagazine
.com/god_article.php?id=7418.

8. Ruth Moon, "Mark Driscoll Addresses Crude Comments,"
Christianity Today, Aug. 1, 2014.

9. Stacey Solie, "Inside Mars Hill's Massive Meltdown," Crosscut, July
16, 2014, http://crosscut.com/2014/07/inside-mars-hills-big
-meltdown/.

10. "Wednesday's Word," Paul Tripp, March 18, 2015. www.paultripp
.com/wednesdays-word/posts/relentless and "The Tornado, the
Lutherans, and Homosexuality," John Piper, August 19, 2009,
Desiring God, www.desiringgod.org/articles/the-tornado-the
-lutherans-and-homosexuality.

11. Kathleen Galek and Matthew Porter, "A Brief Review of Religious
Beliefs in Research on Mental Health and ETAS Theory," *Journal
of Health Care Chaplaincy,* 16 (2010): 58–64.

15. Sin: Pocket Nails and a Mountain of Metaphors

1. Scot McKnight, "Why Doesn't Anybody Talk About Sin?"
Relevant, July 13, 2011, http://archives.relevantmagazine.com/god
/deeper-walk/features/26172-why-doesnt-anybody-talk-about
-sin-anymore?start=1.

2. Exodus 20:5. See also Gary Anderson, *Sin: A History* (New Haven:
Yale University Press, 2009), 3–4.

3. Anderson, *Sin*, 6.

4. Anderson, *Sin*, 7–8.

5. Anderson, *Sin*, 7–8. Anderson notes that this idea is absent in the First Temple period and is likely the result of the influence of Aramaic, which is a language used for commerce and trade.

6. As Dr. Gary Anderson writes, "All of these metaphors can be found in the Bible. But it was not the case that the biblical authors had all these options before them and freely chose among them as the occasion might merit. Quite the opposite was true. During the early periods one particular metaphor dominated, that of sin as a weight. But by the beginning of the Second Temple period a new metaphor emerged that would take center stage, that of sin as a debt. Sin, I wish to claim, does have a history. Near the end of the biblical period, writers are talking about sin in a strikingly different manner." *Sin*, 13.

7. Anderson, *Sin*, 8.

8. Anderson, *Sin*, 9–10.

9. Ľubomír Batka, "Martin Luther's Teaching on Sin," *Oxford Research Encyclopedia of Religion*, December 2016, http://religion.oxfordre.com/view/10.1093/acrefore/9780199340378.001.0001/acrefore-9780199340378-e-373.

10. The last two categories—sin as lawlessness and sin as sickness—roughly mirror those offered by Barbara Brown Taylor, *Speaking of Sin* (Cambridge, MA: Cowley, 2001), 40. I've added sin as "problem" based on my own experiences and observations.

11. Taylor, *Speaking of Sin*, 54.

12. I highly recommend Cornelius Plantiga's book, *Not the Way It's Supposed to Be: A Breviary of Sin* (Grand Rapids, MI: Eerdmans, 1995).

16. *Grace: Umbrellas and Unmerited Favor*

1. Kevin Allen, "The Eastern Orthodox Theology of Grace: An Interview with Fr. Michael Shanbour," *Ancient Faith Ministries,*

November 8, 2016, https://blogs.ancientfaith.com/behind-the
-scenes/2016/11/08/eastern-orthodox-theology-grace-shanbour/.

2. John Piper, "Why Hope? Grace!" Desiring God, April 13, 1986,
www.desiringgod.org/messages/why-hope-grace.

3. This piece is rooted in an ancient definition of the Greek word for
grace, *charis.*

17. Brokenness: Reparative Therapy and Our Aversion to Responsibility

1. "Psychiatry: Homosexuality can be cured," *Time,* February 12,
1965. See also www.theatlantic.com/politics/archive/2015/04/how
-christians-turned-against-gay-conversion-therapy/390570/.

2. Jonathan Merritt, "How Christians Turned Against Gay Conversion Therapy," *The Atlantic,* April 15, 2015. www.theatlantic.com
/politics/archive/2015/04/how-christians-turned-against-gay
-conversion-therapy/390570/.

3. Psalm 34:18

18. Blessed: Hollow Hashtags and Marble Toilets

1. Kate Bowler, "Death, the Prosperity Gospel, and Me," *The New
York Times,* www.nytimes.com/2016/02/14/opinion/sunday
/death-the-prosperity-gospel-and-me.html?_r=0.

2. Laurie Goodstein, "Senator Questioning Ministries on Spending,"
The New York Times, www.nytimes.com/2007/11/07/us/07
ministers.html.

3. Peter J. Reilly, "About That Kenneth Copeland Mansion You Saw
on John Oliver," *Forbes,* August 25, 2015, www.forbes.com/sites
/peterjreilly/2015/08/25/about-that-kenneth-copeland-mansion
-you-saw-on-john-oliver/#7bcd5221d691.

4. Jessica Chasmar, "Televangelists Defend Private Jets: Commercial
Planes Full of 'Demons,'" *Washington Times,* January 5, 2016,
www.washingtontimes.com/news/2016/jan/5/kenneth-copeland
-jesse-duplantis-defend-private-je/.

5. Jazmine Denise Rogers, "Watch Creflo Dollar Respond to $65M Jet Fundraiser Critics: 'You Cannot Curse What God Has Blessed,'" April 23, 2015, http://madamenoire.com/528291/watch-creflo-dollar-responds-to-65m-jet-fundraiser-critics-you-cannot-stop-and-you-cannot-curse-what-god-has-blessed/. (Emphasis added.)

6. Kate Bowler, "Death, the Prosperity Gospel, and Me," *The New York Times,* February 13, 2016, www.nytimes.com/2016/02/14/opinion/sunday/death-the-prosperity-gospel-and-me.html.

7. Jessica Bennett, "Blessed Becomes a Popular Hashtag on Social Media," *The New York Times,* www.nytimes.com/2014/05/04/fashion/blessed-becomes-popular-word-hashtag-social-media.html. Bowler echoes Bennett's sentiments: "#Blessed is the only caption suitable for viral images of alpine vacations and family yachting in barely there bikinis. It says: 'I *totally* get it. I am down-to-earth enough to know that this is crazy.' But it also says: 'God gave this to me. [Adorable shrug.] Don't blame me, I'm blessed.'" "Death, the Prosperity Gospel, and Me."

8. I cannot recommend Kate's work highly enough. For more on her academic research, read *Blessed: A History of the American Prosperity Gospel.* (Oxford: Oxford University Press, 2013). To read about her cancer journey, see *Everything Happens for a Reason: And Other Lies I've Loved* (New York: Random House: 2018).

9. Bowler, "Death, the Prosperity Gospel, and Me." www.nytimes.com/2016/02/14/opinion/sunday/death-the-prosperity-gospel-and-me.html.

19. Neighbor: Mister Rogers and the Global Refugee Crisis

1. Jonathan Merritt, "The Trauma-Filled Tragedy of Syria's Child Refugees," *The Week,* Sept. 9, 2014. http://theweek.com/articles/443963/traumafilled-tragedy-syrias-child-refugees.

2. See Luke 10:25–37.

3. Ree Hines, "Mr. Rogers 'hated' TV—so 45 years ago, he changed it," *Today,* Feb. 19, 2013, www.today.com/popculture/mr-rogers -hated-tv-so-45-years-ago-he-changed-1C8421297.

4. *Revisiting Mister Rogers' Neighborhood: Essays on Lessons About Self and Community,* eds. Kathy Merlock Jackson, Steven M. Emmanuel (Jefferson, NC: McFarland, 2016), 19.

5. See Jonathan Merritt, "Restoration in the Land of Make-Believe: The Legacy of Fred Rogers," *The Huffington Post,* www.huffingtonpost .com/jonathan-merritt/restoration-in-the-land-o_b_863075.html.

6. Jonathan Merritt, "Saint Fred," *The Atlantic,* www.theatlantic .com/politics/archive/2015/11/mister-rogers-saint/416838/.

7. Merritt, "Saint Fred."

8. "Won't you be a good neighbor?" *Christian Science Monitor,* March 23, 1999, www.csmonitor.com/1999/0323/p11s3.html.

20. *Pride: The Self-Esteem Movement and Tiptoe Terms*

1. Will Storr, "The Man Who Destroyed America's Ego," Matter, https://medium.com/matter/ the-man-who-destroyed-americas-ego-94d214257b5.

2. Storr, "The Man Who Destroyed America's Ego."

3. Storr, "The Man Who Destroyed America's Ego."

4. Storr, "The Man Who Destroyed America's Ego."

5. Jessica Tracy, interview by Knowledge @ Wharton staff, "The 'Deadly Sin': The Positive and Negative Power of Pride," November 2, 2016.

6. Genesis 1:31.

21. *Saint: Protestant Holes and Holy Fools*

1. Barbara Brown Taylor, quoted in Jonathan Merritt, "Why Protestants need some saints of our own." Religion News Service, Nov. 4, 2014.

2. "Saints and Angels," Catholic Online, www.catholic.org/saints/.

3. 1 Corinthians 4:10, NLT

22. Confession: Internet Vulnerability and Grace the Doorman

1. Jonathan Merritt, "Put Your Clothes Back On: Oversharing Online Isn't Wise," Religion News Service, http://religionnews.com/2015 /01/20/sharing-online-isnt-always-wise-even-virtual-vomit-goes -viral/.

2. Merritt, "Put Your Clothes Back On."

3. "2014's Word of the Year is Overshare," *NBC News,* www.cbsnews .com/video/2014s-word-of-the-year-is-overshare/.

4. Eleanor Black, "Too Much Information: The Perils of Oversharing Online," Stuff, November 8, 2015, www.stuff.co.nz/life-style /73716713/.
   Too-much-information-The-perils-of-oversharing-online.

5. Katelyn Beaty, "Not All Vulnerability Is Brave," *Christianity Today,* November 2014, www.christianitytoday.com/women/2014 /november/sorry-brene-brown-not-all-vulnerability-is-brave.html.

6. "Why do people overshare online," BBC, www.bbc.com/news /blogs-magazine-monitor-29744828.

7. Brené Brown, *Daring Greatly,* (New York: Avery, 2012) 45–46, (emphasis mine).

8. For example, James 5:16 says, "Confess your sins to each other and pray for each other so that you may be healed."

23. Spirit: Mr. Ghost and the Pronoun Wars

1. Much has been written on the suppression of conservative ideals and viewpoints in institutions of higher ed. For a more thorough exploration, see Kirsten Powers, *The Silencing: How the Left Is Killing Free Speech.*

2. John Piper, "The Frank and Manly Mr. Ryle—The Value of a Masculine Ministry," January 2012, Desiring God, www.desiring god.org/resource-library/conference-messages/the-frank-and-manly -mr-ryle-the-value-of-a-masculine-ministry.

3. Genesis 1:27; Deuteronomy 32:11–12; 32:18; Job 38:8, 29; Psalm 22:9–10; Isaiah 42:14, 49:15; Hosea 13:8 (also see Hosea 11:3–4); Luke 13:34

4. Lauren Winner, *Wearing God* (New York: HarperCollins, 2015), 168.

5. A comment on Song of Songs 8:5, quoted in Winner, *Wearing God,* 141, 169.

6. Winner, *Wearing God,* 27.

7. Lera Boroditsky, "How Does Our Language Shape the Way We Think?" Edge, www.edge.org/conversation/lera_boroditsky-how -does-our-language-shape-the-way-we-think.

8. Lawrence T. White, "Masculine or Feminine? (And Why It Matters)" *Psychology Today* (blog), Sept. 21, 2012, www .psychologytoday.com/us/blog/culture-conscious/201209 /masculine-or-feminine-and-why-it-matters.

9. By listing these masculine and feminine adjectives, I don't mean to imply that these words are ontologically masculine or feminine. Rather, that they are referenced here as cultural descriptors.

10. Sally McFague, *Metaphorical Theology: Models of God in Religious Language* (Minneapolis: Fortress, 1987), 99.

24. Family: Our Changing Households from Munsters to Dunphys

1. Richie Bernardo, "2017's Most Diverse Cities in America," Wallet Hub, May 4, 2017, https://wallethub.com/edu/most-diverse-cities /12690/.

2. Gus Lubin, "Queens Has More Languages Than Anywhere in the World—Here's Where They're Found," Business Insider, February 15, 2017, www.businessinsider.com/queens-languages -map-2017-2.

3. Baby Boomers, for example, were raised in an era during which American society accepted that a family consisted of a breadwin-ning father, a submissive mother who managed the affairs of the house rather than working outside of the home, and some number of well-behaved, biological children. This was the unquestioned norm. Throw in a thirty-year mortgage, a fluffy dog, and a pristine white picket fence, and you have what was considered the picture of perfection and dubbed "the American Dream."

4. Wendy Wang, Kim Parker, and Paul Taylor. "Breadwinner Moms," Pew Research Center, www.pewsocialtrends.org/2013/05/29 /breadwinner-moms/.

5. Jonathan Merritt, "From 'Full House' to 'Modern Family': Ten Shows That Forced Us to Reimagine the American Family," Religion News Service, September 10, 2013, http://religionnews .com/2013/09/10/from-full-house-to-modern-family-ten-shows -that-forced-us-to-reimagine-the-american-family/.

6. As Fitzgerald says, "America just accepted [The Brady Bunch]. After all, the Bradys seemed about as normal as a family could be." Also of note: The character of Mike Brady was a widower, but Schwartz wanted Carol Brady to be depicted as a divorcee. The network objected to this, so Carol's marital past was left open.

7. In television, timing is everything and culture will often resist an idea if it is not yet ready to receive it. The notorious coming-out episode of *Ellen* aired in April of 1997 and was one of the highest rated, but the controversy it created led to the show's eventual cancellation. A mere five years later, Ellen came back with her daytime talk show. The America that once rejected her now celebrated her. Her show generated record ratings and catapulted her back into the limelight. Many of her fans today are unaware of Ellen's previous controversy. Her orientation is now a nonissue. In some ways, *Will & Grace* picked up where *Ellen* left off, and the show's cultural impact lies in its ability to normalize a contentious issue.

8. Thanks in part to the somewhat subtle approach of *Will & Grace,* America began to envision open and unashamed gay and lesbian people as integral to the family. The show's sixteen Emmys and ongoing success in syndication provide a testament to its enduring ability to reach beyond a niche audience of social progressives and influence mainstream Americans.

9. See, for example, 2 Samuel 12:8 and Deuteronomy 25:5.

10. Rodney Clapp, *Family at the Crossroads: Beyond Traditional and Modern Options* (Downers Grove: InterVarsity, 1993), 35.

11. Clapp, *Family at the Crossroads,* 13. The last sixty years have seen rapid change in our understanding of *family,* but as Clapp explains, so did biblical and postbiblical history. The family has taken a number of forms with a range of portraits and iterations since the beginning of time.

25. Lost: Microaggressions and Our Common Condition

1. Amy-Jill Levine, *Short Stories by Jesus: Enigmatic Parables of a Controversial Preacher* (New York: HarperOne, 2015), 36.
2. Levine, *Short Stories by Jesus,* 29. Levine writes, "If any blame is to be assigned in the first two parables, then the shepherd and the woman are at fault, for they 'lost,' respectively, the sheep and the coin."
3. Levine, *Short Stories by Jesus,* 49.
4. Luke 15:7, emphasis mine.

+ In the Beginning Was the Conversation

1. John 1:1
2. George Alexander Kennedy and Glyn P. Norton, eds., *The Cambridge History of Literary Criticism: Volume 3, The Renaissance* (Cambridge: Cambridge University Press, 1989), 45.
3. This English version of Erasmus's translation was provided by Clive Scott, a linguist and professor of European Literature at University of East Anglia. See: http://cornerstonemk.blogspot.com/2009/04/in-2001-i-was-listening-to-radio-4.html. Scott notes that most English translations later reverted to "Word" because of their heavy reliance on certain Church Fathers and Greek philosophy.
4. 2 Corinthians 3:3
5. As Walter Jost and Wendy Olmsted write: "A modern scholar, in command of a treasury of philological research, can only approve Erasmus's choice of *sermo* rather than *verbum* for the translation of the Johannine prologue. *Logos* means speech: a continuous statement, narrative, oration; verbal expression or utterance; a particular utterance or saying; expression, utterance, speech regarded formally.

Both the New Testament and patristic literature in Greek preserve these meanings. Even in the classical lexicon, where other meanings were in ascendency, *logos* signified a phrase, complex term, sentence, or complete statement, in opposition to a discrete word *(verbum)*. It was a continuous statement such as a fable, legend, story, or speech delivered in court or assembly. Rarely meaning a single word, *logos* could never signify grammatically a vocable." *A Companion to Rhetoric and Rhetorical Criticism* (Hoboken, NJ: John Wiley & Sons, 2008) 167–68. See also Marjorie O'Rourke Boyle, "Sermon: Reopening the Conversation on Translating Jn 1,1," *Vigiliae Christianae,* 31, no. 3 (Sept. 1977): 161–68.

6. Kennedy and Norton, *The Cambridge History of Literary Criticism,* 46.

A How-To Guide for Seekers and Speakers

1. Schott's Vocab, "Q and A: The Death of Languages," *The New York Times,* Dec. 16, 2009, https://schott.blogs.nytimes.com/2009/12/16/q-and-a-the-death-of-languages/.

About the Author

Jonathan Merritt is one of America's most prolific and popular religion writers. He is currently a contributing writer for *The Atlantic,* contributing editor for *The Week,* and senior columnist for *Religion News Service.* Jonathan has published more than 3,500 articles in respected outlets such as *USA Today, The Washington Post,* BuzzFeed, *Christianity Today,* and *The New York Times.* As a respected voice on religion and politics, he has been interviewed on ABC World News, CNN, Fox News, MSNBC, PBS, NPR, and CBS's *60 Minutes.*

Jonathan is the author of multiple books, including the critically acclaimed *Jesus Is Better Than You Imagined.* He has collaborated on or ghostwritten more than fifty others, with several titles landing on the *New York Times, Wall Street Journal,* and *USA Today* bestsellers lists.

Named one of "30 young influencers reshaping Christian leadership" by *Outreach* magazine, Jonathan is now a sought after speaker at colleges, conferences, and churches. He holds two graduate degrees in religion and resides in Brooklyn, New York.

To learn more about Jonathan's work or to receive his popular weekly newsletter—"The Faith and Culture 5"—visit www.JonathanMerritt .com.

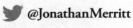 @JonathanMerritt

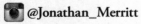 @Jonathan_Merritt

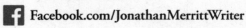 Facebook.com/JonathanMerrittWriter